YOUR LOVED ONE MAY BE DYING?

by

JESUS OF NAZARETH
&
Fr. Francis Pompei ofm

OVERWHELMED? THOUGHTS AND EMOTIONS OUT OF CONTROL?

"STOP IT! I am with you. So start reading."

DEDICATION

To all of YOU reading this book who are probably overwhelmed and your thoughts and emotions are out of control because your loved one may be dying

INTRODUCTION

I suggest that you skip the listing of the Chapters on the next page and view it later after you read Chapter 1.

Go right to Chapter 1 and let the Lord calm you down and start walking with Him through everything that is on the road ahead for you and your loved one.

When you see **JESUS:** This is Jesus talking to you.

So, as Jesus says on the Cover, **"Start reading"**.

COPYRIGHT
All rights reserved

No part of this publication may be reproduced, stored in a retrieval system or transmitted in any form or by any means, mechanical, electronic, photocopying, recording or otherwise without the prior written permission of the publisher.

EDITOR: Trish Pompei

TABLE OF CONTENTS

CHAPTER 1	"I AM WITH YOU"	5
CHAPTER 2	SUFFERING AND TRUST	20
CHAPTER 3	VISITING YOUR LOVED ONE AFTER YOU GET THE CALL	34
CHAPTER 4	THE FAMILY GATHERS	43
CHAPTER 5	TOUGH DECISIONS AND LETTING GO	45
CHAPTER 6	DEATH: WHAT TO DO	49
CHAPTER 7	WHEN YOUR LOVED ONES BODY'S DEATH BEGINS	58
CHAPTER 8	GRADUATION: THE REAL 'PASSOVER'	60
CHAPTER 9	DEVASTATED AND SURREAL, BUT MUCH TO DO	70
CHAPTER 10	VISITING THE CEMETERY	82
CHAPTER 11	WHEN EVERY ONE GOES HOME	88
CHAPTER 12	CLEANING THEIR ROOM AND BELONGINGS	90

CHAPTER 13	NO FAMILY AND NO ONE TO REMEMBER	92
CHAPTER 14	GRIEVING	96
CHAPTER 15	WHAT WILL HEAVEN BE LIKE?	108
CHAPTER 16	A GIFT FOR YOU FROM KEATON AND MARY GRACE	120
CHAPTER 17	TIME WITH JESUS PRAYERS COMPILATION	124

Prayer When You Are Overwhelmed	124
Visiting Your Loved One	127
Be My Voice For Your Loved One	132
Family Visit With Loved One Prayer	135
Family Service To Guide Your Loved One	137
Graduation Prayer	139
Prayer When Leaving After They Passed	146
Viewing Your Loved One At The Wake	147
Short Prayer Before You Leave The Wake	149
Visiting The Cemetery	150
A Prayer Before Cleaning Their Room	156

CHAPTER 1
"I AM WITH YOU"

Peace be with you! It's me, Jesus. Yes, it's me, your Lord and most of all, your friend. Two thousand years ago I said that I would never abandon you and I would be with you every day until the end of time.

So here I am. It's really me.

If you are reading this then you are frightened, overwhelmed and panicked about your loved one's life threatening news. By now the floodgates of your mind have opened wide and many negative thoughts and half- truths have entered your mind that is spinning out of control, and your emotions and feelings are exploding off the charts.

SLOW DOWN, and if you are looking for answers and help from me, then take a deep breath... Make a choice to stay with me and keep reading.

Remember when I said that while you are in your physical earthly bodies you will suffer, but not to be afraid, I meant it. The reason you are afraid, worried, and devastated is not because of me. Satan is filling your mind with these thoughts and lies because he is the 'father of lies' and was so from the beginning.

I am the Truth that you are looking for and that's why I am here because I promised and said I would be. What's keeping you from experiencing me right now are all the negative, half-truths and lies that evil is putting in your mind and with them all those awful emotions of fear, worrying, doubt, and maybe even despair that's causing you to have an anxiety and panic attack. Because of this you can't think or dwell on anything else. Evil has, without your realizing, captured and imprisoned your mind to think and continue to dwell on the suffering of your loved one and yours.

Add to this that you have been abruptly taken from your daily routine, secure and somewhat safe life, and thrust into 'HELL', with nothing and maybe no one who can make it all go away and disappear. All this is from Satan and Evil and keeping you from experiencing me here with you.

I not only know where you are at, but I too experienced it on the cross when I cried out in a loud voice, "Father, why have you abandoned me."

Yes, the Son of God, me, succumbed to the temptations and attacks of Satan. So, don't think that I am in Heaven and far removed and unaware of what you are going through. My Resurrected physical body is in heaven, but I am right here with you and always have been.

So, don't let Satan and Evil do this to you and keep you from me as I didn't let him keep me from the Father. I focused off my suffering by choosing to call out to Him with Trust by saying, "Father into your hands I commend my Spirit.

Enough words for the time being. I want to not only

teach you, but have you experience me helping you to let go of your anxiety by just being with me. So, relax and let's pray.

If you have a Crucifix, sit in front of it, and just look at me on the cross for 30 sec. or more. It will not only help you by seeing the Unconditional Love I have for you, but experience what is driving me from moment to moment, to endure my suffering and Satan attacking me with Fear.

<u>Pray with me now, and let me guide you to the Peace I promised you.</u>

Evil is attacking you as it did me on the cross and when my good friend Lazarus' physical body died. Evil is tempting you to doubt that I am with you and doing nothing to help, and your fear and suffering will never end.

Calm down and let me help you, and together we will stop the vicious circle.

Slowly Repeat My Words, and let them relax your mind and body little by little, so you can only focus on being here, just you and me...

- Be Still and Know that I am God.... (Pause 30 sec. close your eyes)

- Be Still and Know that I am... (Pause 30 sec. close your eyes)

- Be Still and Know... (Pause 30 sec. close your eyes)

- Be Still... (Pause 30 sec. close your eyes)

- Just Be... (Pause 30 sec. close your eyes)

Trust me now, by praying these words **slowly** with all your faith, mind, and Soul.

- **"Your power, Jesus, is greater than the powers of Evil and Lies that are attacking me."**

- **"In Your name, Jesus, and by the power of your blood, I bind and cast out Fear, Worry, Anxiety, Doubt and Despair."**

- **"Evil, you have no power over me. I belong to Jesus"** (Pause 15 sec.)

- **"Lord, I'm tired and surrender everything to you. Give me peace of mind and rest."**

Imagine the Holy Spirit and my unconditional love
is embracing you, **because it is.**

Close your eyes and enjoy peace of mind and rest. Just keep choosing to be here with me and think positive and good thoughts, like all the people who love you. There's no rush, so take your time. **Think of them one by one and enjoy their presence when you do...**

Now, no more thinking, no more praying... just **'Being'**... together... me with you... and you with me.
(Take as much time as you need)

Welcome back. You did it."

Now keep reading and listen to me, because little by little you will worry less and focus on me with you. Then you will start experiencing peace in the midst of all the insanity you will have to deal with on the road ahead. That's why I said, "Come to me all you who are laboring and heavy burdened, and **I WILL GIVE YOU REST** and **PEACE** of mind."

What I am going to teach you next is real important to help you find peace, hope and the strength you will need to not only heal yourself, but also free your loved one from their fear, by **Loving** and **Guiding** them through their suffering and when they leave their physical bodies.

What greater gift could you give them than your love, to celebrate their life and deliver them from their fears and worry? Then you can lead them step by step to pass out of their physical body and be set free, whether conscious or in a coma, to come home to where the Father and I created them.

So, focus on that for some 'GOOD NEWS', and there is more to come that you can't even imagine how great it is.

THE REAL TRUTH

Suffering and death are not the real enemy as Satan and Evil have taught you. I'm going to repeat this so you can start **undoing** what you have been seduced into believing is the TRUTH. It is **NOT**. Because you have been taught to think this way, you always get trapped into the vicious circle and the downward spiral of Doubt, Self-Pity, Hopelessness, and Despair.

STOP IT, and discipline your mind with the real **TRUTH**.

"It is your **FEAR** of suffering and death that is the **ENEMY**!"

I am going to repeat this again so that you will not only understand it, but start changing the way you think and start changing what you say to yourself and others that can liberate you from the vicious circle and downward spiral that you are in right now.

"It is your **FEAR of suffering and death** that is the **ENEMY**"!

I want you to think about this for a minute. Let me help you.

- You are afraid of the physical pain your loved one is experiencing.

- You wish you could make it go away and stop.

- You are afraid of the pain that they are experiencing now may get worse.

- You are afraid if there is nothing you, doctors, or anyone can do to help, heal, restore, or prevent them from dying.

- You are afraid if what they and you are feeling will only get worse and never go away.

- You are frightened and terrified what you will do without them if they die.

- You are afraid of never seeing them ever again or feeling their Love and how wonderful, safe, and loved you always feel when you are with them.

- Lastly, you are terrified of what you are experiencing right now, Powerless, Desperate, Alone, and Numb.

By me putting these thoughts and feelings before you, you are probably ready to explode. If you are, then **STOP** reading and let them out.

Cry, weep and even Wail if you have to, but imagine I am holding you, just as Mary, Martha and I held each other at the death of their brother and my friend, Lazarus.

Crying and letting it out is one of the great gifts I gave you. So cry and cry as long and often as you need to and give it all to me... Don't let anyone tell you not to cry.

Tears are good and show the great Love you have for your loved one.

At the end of tears are release, peace and Love, until you are attacked again and download evil back into your mind by thinking and dwelling on the Lies.

Let me teach you something important that will help you now and in the future.

Satan and Evil has infected not only our physical bodies with sin, suffering and death, but also our Minds by giving them the ability and power to know both **Good** and **Evil**. We all download these thoughts by **thinking** about them and **dwelling** on them.

That's how Fear, which is Evil and Satan's greatest power gets into your mind. And that's how it got into me in the agony in the garden, when they scourged me, and on the cross when my body was dying. As I said before, the real enemy is not suffering and death but your fear of them, as it was mine.

The good news for you right now is, that just as I conquered my fears from moment to moment, I will not only help you conquer yours, but help you to conquer your loved ones and be an instrument to give them peace in the midst of their temptation and suffering.

This is why I came into the world, to give you the power to overcome evil and give you hope beyond your imagination. As my friend and brother St. Paul said he not only believed this, but experienced it.

- "Nothing can separate us from the love of my Lord Jesus the Christ. Will anguish, or distress or persecution, or famine, nakedness, peril, or the sword?

- No, in all these things, we are more than conquerors through Him who loves us.

- For I am convinced that neither DEATH, nor life, nor angels, nor principalities, nor present things, nor future things, nor powers, nor height, nor depth, nor any other creature will be able to separate us from the Love of God in Christ Jesus my Lord." (Romans 8:31)

If fear is your enemy right now, then let's start to deliver you from it. Two thousand years ago I said "Love dispels fear and where there is Fear, Love has not yet been experienced."

Besides experiencing the Unconditional Love I had for you on the cross, I want you to **stop reading** and spend as long as you need remembering your wonderful memories of Love, closeness, and fun that you had and have with your loved one. Use your imagination and memory and re- experience them, laugh, and enjoy them.

These memories are part of your healing and hope, not only now, but will also be for your loved one when you share them with him/her. These will last for all eternity because they **ARE** the **LOVE** you have for each other.

Take your time, go way back, remember, re-live, enjoy, and experience them again...

(When you finish, start reading and listening to me again so I can teach you how to confront and deliver yourself from the evil that is and will keep attacking you and your loved one who is most likely vulnerable to the negative thoughts and lies and is terrified.)

What will set you free from the Fear and anxiety attacks is the **TRUTH**. You need to know that the Truth is not only a thought or idea, but a **PERSON**, and that Person is me, your Lord who loves you. That's why I said, "I myself am the Truth, Life itself, and the Way to find them."

Put simply, by your coming to me like you did with your parents when you were frightened, you have come to me and I will Love the Fear and Worrying right out of you.

The depth of how much you are suffering now is because you grew up and became less and less dependent on me. Instead you have been seduced into believing you are and can be in control of your life and take care of yourself. This is how evil has distracted and kept you from faith and Trust in me, replaced by a false sense of security.

Now you know why I said "You must become like a little child in order to enter the Kingdom of God." In other words, re-learn how to Trust and come to me first and throughout your day, like when you were a child. The good news is that you are doing it right now because you came to me by picking up this book and spending time with me. I want you to know you are giving me great Joy.

To experience the power of this Love to heal and transform your sadness into joy, take a moment and remember some special moments when you ran to your parent or loved one who embraced, comforted you and made you forget about your problem, feel safe and loved.

Stop reading, take as much time as you need and enjoy. This is what heaven will be like and so much greater by far....

(When you finish)

Another lie that Evil is telling you that is causing you much of your anxiety is that sometimes you are tempted to doubt that I can and desire to walk with you through this. I can and will, if you just continue to read and **Trust** me.

I want you to memorize my **Truths** so you can start using them to dispel and replace the Lies. The more you do this the easier it gets and the more natural it will become.

Finally, you will put a '**Filter**' on your mind and little by little replace the evil that you have been programed to download and think about.

LIES

- Death is the end of my loved one's life.

- The tests will be positive— I know it. They will never endure this.

- Why is God punishing them?

- What's the use of praying to you Lord, if you're not answering?

TRUTH:
- "Don't be afraid or let your heart be troubled. Trust in God and trust in me." (Jn. 14:27)

- "You and your loved one are afraid because you are not experiencing love, instead are focused on the suffering and death. Love will dispel your fear." (1 Jn. 4:18)

- "While you are in the world you will suffer (and your bodies will die), but don't be afraid, for I overcame my fear of Suffering and Death and will be with you in yours." (Jn. 16:33)

SUFFERING LIES
- I will never be able to go through it.

- It will always hurt this badly and even get worse.

- Where is God, and why me?

- I can't take it anymore.

- I won't be able to do the things I use to. What's the use of living?

- It is so frustrating. Will it ever stop?

- I don't understand why we have to suffer for so long. Life is hell.

TRUTH:
- Do not be discouraged; rather, although their outer self (physical body) is wasting away, their

Soul and Spirit is being renewed day by day and will pass over to Eternal Life." (2 Cor. 4:16)

- "Their momentary suffering that you are dwelling on is producing for them right now an eternal glory beyond all comparison, so look beyond their physical body and look to what is unseen, the person who you love; for their body that you are seeing is transitory and passing away, but what is unseen, their Spirit is eternal." (2 Cor. 4:18)

- "Your loved one is sharing and experiencing the suffering and temptation to be afraid that I endured. I promise you, they will share in my resurrection as will you when you leave your body and come home to where you were created and see them again forever." (Rom. 8:17)

DEATH LIES:
- They are dying; last breath, no heart-beat, dead, wake, funeral, buried and forgotten.

- I will never see them ever again or experience the way they always responded, a smile, comforting word or hug.

- This is it. They are never getting out of this one and neither am I. It's what I have always dreaded and now it's happening.

- I feel alone and abandoned by God.

TRUTH:
- "Do not let your heart be troubled. Have faith in God; have faith in me. In my Father's house there are many dwelling places. At the moment they leave their body I will take them to myself, so that where I am they also may be." (Jn. 14:1)

I am begging you to read and re-read the TRUTH. Not only read them and believe in them, but keep doing it until you experience me with you now, yes, right now, with and in you, giving you the answers that you seek to find moments of peace, finally peace. The safest place to be is with me as you are now, and not just now, but in everything that you will have to go through with your loved one.

So, here's what to do and say continually when being dragged down by the lies. Say **NO** to the **LIES** and immediately speak the **TRUTH** that you now know and then say,

"Lord, I'm going to trust in you anyway."

This will be the hardest thing for you to do as it was for me, but just imagine me on the cross experiencing and feeling what you are before you say it. When you finish your prayers and devotions from now on, talk to me as your friend and listen to me as you have been by reading my words. And remember, I Love you, always have and always will.

TRUST and your **WILL** are your gateway to the peace, healing and the hope that you and your loved one are looking for. It is and will be that most difficult choice you will have to make from moment to moment, even though it's as simple as saying,

"Lord, I TRUST in YOU anyway!"

Just remember, I believe in you and am counting on you to pray and Trust this way. I had to do it for my whole earthly life, even with my last breath, and so will YOU. The point here is that there is **no magic prayer or pill that will cure and make all suffering go away**.

I am the 'Gate' and the 'Way' through yours and your loved ones fear of what's on the road ahead. I told you and will tell you again, it's greater than anything you could ever imagine.

All of your worrying is a waste of time and will change nothing. By doing something you like to do and getting connected with people who love you is a necessary part of not only bringing you peace of mind, but life and joy.

Always remember, it's **LOVE** that dispels your Fear. So let people in and watch what happens. Continue reading for more good news about how you and I can really help your family, loved ones, and especially those who are suffering and getting ready to graduate.

I love you... always have and always will.

CHAPTER 2
SUFFERING AND TRUST

SUFFERING IS AN OPPORTUNITY TO GROW IN TRUST
Article by Fr. Francis Pompei ofm

You have heard it said or probably said it yourself, that "Life is Hell." My guess is that all of us have felt this way at some time or another, because of all the suffering and death in the world from the beginning of humankind. To put it simply, somehow superior beings, fallen angels (according to Scripture) or other conscious beings with divine knowledge rebelled against God, chose physical reality, lusted after human women (Forbidden fruit) and interfered with our DNA. This affected our minds and bodies as well all physical reality.

"All creation groans for the salvation of the Lord." (Rom. 8:19-23)

Jesus said, "You have only one teacher", so we must be in school and Jesus is our Teacher. This is not an analogy, but the truth, according to Jesus and the Holy Spirit who will teach us all things.

God created our Consciousness, Mind, and Will in Heaven (The Spirit World). Then He sent and bonded us with the physical bodies that our parents co-created with God, but to do what? Why couldn't we stay in Heaven and be perfectly happy, instead of being in these bodies that suffer and die? Why do we need to go to school for?

THE ANSWER:

To learn and grow! We can learn and grow more here than we can in Heaven or the Spirit World. Why? Because there is both Good and Evil, Sin, Suffering, Fear, Loneliness, and then Death... All of these require making decisions. By paying attention to the Teacher (Jesus and the Holy Spirit), we learn what to do and how to do it to become all that we were created to be.

Let me put some reality on this. We spent the first five or six years of our existence attached to our mothers and caregivers all day every day. They packed our lunch one day, put us on a strange bus with a strange driver with 30 strange kids, and then went to a strange building called 'school', and Mommy didn't come with us. What kind of mother would do that to their child?

Then it got worse. We were marched into a room with 20 more strange kids and a strange person that was not Mommy but called "Teacher." Worst of all is that Mommy left us there alone for almost six hours.

No wonder some kids were hitting the teacher, screaming for Mommy, and punching each other. I thought that Mommy loved me. If she really loved me, why did she send me to HELL!

Is this starting to make sense to you? **LIFE IS NOT HELL. LIFE IS SCHOOL**. For the same reason that our parents sent us to school, God has put us here to learn how to make our own decisions between good and evil, right and wrong, love and hate, greed and generosity, but also to learn the life skills necessary to trust the Lord and deal with problems, suffering and fear.

SUMMARY: Now we know who we are and why God sent us here and bonded us with the physical bodies our parents produced. That is— to go to school. Everything that you and I experience while we are in these physical bodies is being in school. As long as our bodies exist, we are still in school.

Therefore, life is school, and all that happened, is happening, and will happen (good or bad) is an opportunity to **LEARN** and **TRUST**.

Memorize this last sentence.

SO, HERE ARE THE STEPS TO TRUST

No matter what thoughts are in your mind, and no matter how intense your feelings and emotions are,

1. Choose (Use your Will) to focus off of them, the problem, the fear, and what is tempting you.

2. Focus on Jesus with you by simply saying "Lord."

3. Keep choosing to stay focused and say NO to your negative thoughts, feelings and emotions.

4. Rest in His presence, whether you feel Him or not, until you experience peace of mind.

5. Replace your negative thoughts, half-truths, and lies that are in your mind causing your fears, worries, and stress with the Truth and presence of the Lord **RIGHT THERE WITH YOU**.

6. Then do His **will** no matter what you think or feel, constantly aware that He is with you, giving you strength and power to deal with anything.

TRUST THROUGH THE WORD OF GOD: When my Sister Trish faced cancer and surgery she was overcome by fear and worry. She initially asked the Lord for a miracle. When her fear intensified and she became more anxious, she opened her Bible and read words of Jesus that jumped off the page, as if Jesus was right there saying them to her personally.

"While you are in the world you will suffer, but don't be afraid, for I am with you. Trust in God and Trust in me."

She prayed for healing but prayed for the **GRACE TO TRUST** in Jesus and **LET GO OF HER FEAR** by **NOT** dwelling on her cancer and surgery. Instead she focused on the Lord with her and on doing things she would ordinarily do to keep her attention from centering on her cancer. **It was not magic**, because that's not how Trust works.

She was still tempted and attacked by fear, but kept choosing to tell Jesus she trusted Him, and she let go. Little by little, the grace she asked for was given to her, because she experienced peace and less and less fear and worry.

The day of her surgery, two of her friends and I were waiting for the doctors to call her down. We prayed with her and again she simply said, "I trust in you, Jesus. Your

Will be done." When we finished, my sister who has a great wit, made us laugh with funny one-liners about her surgery. All of us, my sister included, felt absolutely no fear or worry at that moment.

When the doctor and nurse walked in, we were having a full belly laugh. Later the doctor told my sister that in all his years doing surgery, he never experienced someone so unafraid and overcome with laughter as they wheeled her into surgery. My sister told him that Jesus told her to trust Him, and she did. Does Jesus communicate and reveal his will for us through His words? You bet He does. Just ask my sister.

HOPE OR DESPAIR
(Steve has had ALS for ten years which is incredible in itself. He has been paralyzed from the neck down and unable to take care of any of his bodily needs. He is totally dependent for 10 years on his wife and a care taker who comes only once or twice a week. Steve has offered the following to all who are suffering seriously. How do you find hope instead of negative evil thoughts leading you down the path to depression and despair?)

STEVE:
Suddenly, being thrust into having (too much) time on your hands allows an opportunity for creativity, introspection, spiritual growth, reconnecting, and catching up.

These are some activities from my experience that have been most helpful.

- **Make a conscious decision to look forward to good things only.** "I'm looking forward to..." Whether it is a picnic, visiting, or good food, I've learned to have something good on my mind to anticipate. Always have something good to look forward to.

- **Choose to have and maintain a positive attitude**. I have much to be thankful for, and most importantly, I feel loved. **Surround yourself with love, both given and received - but especially given. There are great things to come and I have a lot to give.**

- **Make the effort to share emotional connections with friends and family, counting your blessings not troubles**. What a gift to do this, because it will catapult you to happiness!

- **Open your heart to receive prayers from others**. Myself, I pray for **understanding, perseverance, and health**. I know that's a lot to ask given the blessings already bestowed.

- **I have continued to stay as active as possible. Boredom and frustration opens the doors of opportunity. Being creative helps.** I love to be creative, find solutions, and make improvements.

- **There have been moments of anxiousness which are tough to talk myself down from**. Mild doses of medication help. I have also experienced uncontrollable panic attacks. Not fun. They have only occurred at times when my airway was compromised and I couldn't breathe. **I've learned how to prevent that problem by triple checking my surroundings for vulnerability.**

- **I have realized great benefits from my faith in Jesus, spiritual readings and prayer** as far as strengthening my resolve to be a better man and Christian.

- **I am sure that prayer has given me the strength and mental capacity to maintain a positive attitude.** I have much to be thankful for, and most importantly, I feel loved, especially by my wife who has personally taken care of all my needs for the past ten years with all the incredible frustration, anxiety, stress, and patience required. All our friends and me included can't imagine what she has had to endure these past ten years.

- **There are great things to come** and I have a lot to give. And I encourage all of you who are reading this, to look beyond the suffering and feel free to learn and do what I have done and continue to do. God will bless you as he has me with both hope and happiness. I will pray for you and hope you will pray for me. Oh, I forgot, our reward in Heaven will be great when we graduate from these bodies.

God bless,
Steve

UNCLE TONY: A PERSONAL STORY TO FIND PEACE OF MIND BY TRUSTING IN THE LORD

My uncle Tony was lying on a hospital bed in the middle of his living room at home, in pain and dying. Uncle Tony was not my biological uncle, but I chose him to be my sponsor for Confirmation, because he was one of my favorite uncles. He was a real man of faith and brought my cousins to church all of the time, completing novenas, the Rosary, Stations of the Cross on Fridays, and Mass on Sundays.

When I came in and sat down next to him, he smiled and said he was glad to see me. I asked him how he was doing and if he was afraid. To this day, I will never forget what he said and the experience I had of the Lord right there with and in Him.

He said, "No Francis, I'm not afraid. I've trusted the Lord my whole life, and He got me through everything. No, Francis, I'm not afraid, because all I have to do is **TRUST HIM ONE MORE TIME**."

There it was, right in front of me in my Uncle—Peace of Mind, courage and waiting to go home. Then, with his Italian wit, he said, "The only thing I wish (and it's frustrating the hell out of me) is for this damn body to let me go." That's what we prayed for—that his body would die so that he could finally leave his school building and graduate. And that he did, in peace, at one with his God.

From now on, for the rest of your earthly life, say it to the Lord at the beginning of your day, and the moment you are facing a problem. Be open to learn whatever it is, good or bad. This is the new paradigm or context that you need to discern and measure everything with. The real truth is that Life is School and this will dispel all the confusion, frustration, and temptations to doubt God. Now you will know who and what you are, and why you are here. This is great news, if you ask me.

After the initial shock of Mommy abandoning you when she sent you to Kindergarten, you gradually adjusted to the strangeness and strangers by listening to the teacher, and you were no longer afraid but actually wanted to go to school and learn. Makes sense to me! The following chart will explain what life is about in the context of being in school and what God wants us to learn while we are here.

LIFE IS NOT HELL, LIFE IS SCHOOL

THE SCHOOL BUILDING	**OUR PHYSICAL BODIES** God bonds our Consciousness, Mind & Will with our physical bodies that our parents produced. The same reason our mothers sent us to school.

THE DEGREE WE ARE TO GRADUATE WITH	**TRUST IN GOD** is the reason we are in school, **not** to be **perfect.** • "Thy will be done" (Mt. 6:10) • "Trust in God" (Jn. 14:1) No matter what we think or feel, with our Will, choose to let go of control and TRUST instead. (Do it the Lord's way.)
SUBJECTS TO GROW IN EVERY DAY	**UNCONDITIONAL LOVE**: "Love God with your whole heart, mind, and soul." (Mt. 22:37) **GENEROSITY**: "The Blessings you have received, give them freely. I was hungry and you gave me something to eat…" (Mt. 25) **FORGIVENESS**: "Love your enemies," "Forgive us our trespasses, as we forgive those who trespass against us." (Lk. 6:35)
TEACHER	**JESUS**: "You have only one Teacher. The Holy Spirit will teach you all things." (Jn. 14:26) Learn to think like Jesus and live like Jesus.

	"Do not conform yourself to this World but put on the mind of Christ." This requires working on this 24/7, as long as we are in these bodies. (School)
BEING A GOOD STUDENT	**PAY ATTENTION**- Train your brain. If you don't, You won't learn. Focus on Jesus, and not the problem, lies, negative thoughts, half-truths. If you do not discipline and train your mind to do this, it's like looking out the window in school. You won't learn what to do or how to deal with your problems or suffering. Then fear will take over. "You cannot serve God and money." (Power/Pleasure/ Sports, etc.) (Mt. 6:24) "If anyone would be my disciple, you must **DENY** your very selves, pick up your cross, and follow me." (Lk. 9:23)

DAILY HOMEWORK, EXERCISES DRILLS	**SACRIFICING FOR OTHERS** To learn God's way of thinking and living through acts of love, generosity, forgiveness, sacrificing what you want or want to do, for the sake of others— It's called LOVE.
POP QUIZZES	**SMALL PROBLEMS**: are Opportunities to learn how to Trust by doing it. "If you TRUST me in small things, I will place you over greater." (Lk. 16:10)
TESTS	**MORE SERIOUS PROBLEMS AND SUFFERING**: Opportunities to learn how to deal with Fear-Worry-Doubt by trusting in Jesus. "Nothing can separate us from the love of God in Christ Jesus my Lord, for in all things we are more than conquerors." (Rom. 8:31)

RECESS	**WHEN THINGS ARE GOING WELL YOU ARE AT PEACE** because you are learning how to deal with problems, fear, and suffering, together with Jesus.
	"I have come to give you Peace of Mind and give you JOY and make your experience of joy complete." (Jn. 14:27)
VACATION	**LONGER PERIODS OF PEACE** This is the result of your trusting the Lord and becoming aware of Him more and more when dealing with life, and living His way. This is a foretaste of Heaven. Get ready for EXAMS. Then move up a grade! Hooray!
FINAL EXAMS When your Physical Body dies	**GRADUATION:** Your Soul, Consciousness, Mind that are not physical leaves your body and Jesus takes you home to Heaven where God created you, Eternal life. **CONGRATULATIONS! YOU DID IT!**

DEATH IS GRADUATION ACCORDING TO JESUS

- "Our citizenship is in Heaven." (Phil. 3:20)

- "Unless the seed falls to the ground and dies, it remains just a seed, but if it falls to the ground and dies, it will bear much fruit." (Jn.12:24)

- "I am the resurrection and life. Anyone who believes in me, when your physical body dies, I will raise you up. (Your Soul, Consciousness, Mind, and Will that I created, to come back home with me forever) (Jn. 11:17)

- "Therefore we do not lose heart, but though our outer body is decaying, our inner spirit is being renewed day by day. Our suffering and affliction is TEMPORARY (School) and producing for us an eternal HOME (Graduation-New Life), and a glory far beyond all comparison.

- "While we do not look at the things which are seen, (Things of the world and physical reality- pleasure, entertainment, power, money, possessions, etc.) but at the things which are not seen (Jesus with/in Us). The things which are seen are temporal and passing away, but the things which are not seen, are eternal." (2 Cor.4:18)

CHAPTER 3
VISITING YOUR LOVED ONE AFTER YOU GET THE CALL

VISITING YOUR LOVED ONE

JESUS:

If you think I have no idea what goes through your mind when you are on your way to visit your loved one who is suffering and whose body is dying, you are mistaken.

When I got word that my good friend Lazarus had died, it was an overwhelming feeling of emptiness, and now that I was in an earthly body knew for the first time what a broken heart felt like. Here were some of my thoughts, and my guess is some of them are yours.

- You will see their bodies in pain maybe, and anguish in their face along with a certain fear in their eyes.

- You will never see them full of life, whole, and healthy again.

- You will never see their smile or feel their touch ever again that you have been so accustomed to.

- They will no longer be at your holiday table or hear the sound of their voice and feel their embrace.

- You will no longer have them at your family's special events and you will miss them terribly and don't even want to think about it.

- There will be no more memories to create when they leave.

- It all feels so unreal, like you are in a very dark space in your soul and there is no light at the end of this, or a way out.

These were my thoughts and feelings when I got word that my friend Lazarus was dead. The result of downloading and thinking about them has and is most likely why you don't know what to do, say, or how you can truly help your loved one through their suffering with Hope and Love.

Here are the Truths that will not only set you free from all the awful thoughts and feelings of not knowing what to do or say, but liberate your Loved One from their fears, give them the hope of what's really happening to them, Graduation and not death, and most of all feel your Love, and you theirs.

- The minute the negative thoughts above enter your mind, say it, shout it, and if you have to scream **NO** to them, do it. Tell them you are no longer and **NOT** going to think about them, instead say to me, **"LORD"** and turn your attention to me, because that's where I am and have been waiting for you to call upon me.

- Then, remember what you have been taught, that you will **not** focus on what your loved one looks like, or if they are in a hospital, nursing home, or hospice, the machines, caretakers and any thoughts that the situation evil might use to keep attacking your mind.

- Look beyond what you see to what is unseen, that is the 'One you love' who is in their body. Their Spirit, Soul, their Consciousness are totally intact whether they are alert, unconscious, or in a coma.

- Now, just be with, talk to them, and treat them as you would if they weren't suffering. This in itself will give them the comfort and assurance that they are OK in the present.

- After you share stories, ask them what are some of the thoughts going through their head and what they are feeling.

- Listen and discern what might be controlling their minds and attacking them: Are they afraid, worried, angry with God, guilty and feeling there is no hope.

- Share with them what I have taught you about fear, suffering, and death. Tell them the Truth and use my words to dispel the lies that may be frightening them.

- Next, get them connected with me right there with you, because that's what I'm waiting for you to do. The way to do this is to invite them to pray and talk to me.

- Bless yourself, then ask to be aware of my presence there with you. (Pause 10 sec. to give yourselves time for your mind to do this.)

"Lord it's good to be with you."

- Then pray and ask for healing and deliverance from fear of suffering and what's in their future.

PRAY:

"Lord, I pray and ask first for a miracle and extraordinary healing for _____.

Secondly, I pray for full and total healing if it is going to take time, days, weeks, whatever. In the meantime I ask that you give patience, courage and strength to endure any pain or suffering until he/she is healed. Give them faith and trust in you from moment to moment when they are tempted to doubt and worry about their future.

I pray that you will bless all of _____ 's caregivers and give them the wisdom and gifts to help in_____'s healing.

Lastly, for those things that will not pass away, I ask that you continually deliver, bind and cast out all those negative thoughts and lies that evil will attack him/her with.

Finally Jesus, you said that Love dispels Fear. I join my Love to yours Jesus, and all those who Love _____. Open your mind and heart _____ and experience the embrace of our love for you.
(Pause for 15- 30 sec. while softly saying over and over, "Thank you Jesus")

Hold their hand, look each other while praying the words I taught you. OUR FATHER... Amen!

(Give a sign of peace, an embrace, a kiss and say,)

"Remember_____, the Lord is right here and Loves you, and so do I.

- Now just visit, talk, and tell stories.

- If they are unconscious or in a coma say, do all the above steps, because their Consciousness, Soul, and Mind understands everything you are saying and doing.

- If you want to stay longer and they are in a coma, sleeping, or unconscious, bring a book, music, sit next to the bed, hold their hand and read in a soft calming voice. Every once in a while, if appropriate, wet a face towel with cool water, fold it and put it on their forehead and even gently wash their face and neck. Doing these things will let them know they are not alone and you and the Lord are still there with them.

- Then, both you and your loved one will experience what I said 2000 years ago.

"Come to me all you who labor and are heavy burdened and I will give you rest and peace."

- Stay in the present there with your loved one and enjoy it.

"I will never abandon you, so Trust and never abandon me."

BE MY VOICE FOR YOUR LOVED ONE WHEN YOU VISIT

(To replace the thoughts that may be causing your loved one to be afraid or worried, read the Truth whether they are awake, unconscious or in a coma.)

YOU:

Lord, you created me and gave me my voice. Use my voice to deliver_____ from any fears he/she may have, heal and give them hope and most of all know that they are not alone and that we love them.

I pray that you_____ will not hear my voice, but experience Jesus' voice not only speaking to you, but is right here and will walk with you through this.

Lord, make me an instrument of your healing and hope.

- "Though you are walking through the valley of darkness, fear no evil, for I am with you."

- "Do not let your hearts be troubled. Have faith in God and have faith in me."

- "Your citizenship is in heaven where I created you. It is where you came from and when you leave your body, I will take you home."

- "In my Father's house there are many dwelling places, not only for you, but for all those who believe in me."

- "I will change your lowly body to be like my

resurrected and glorified body. "

- "When I said while you are in the world and in your physical body you will suffer, but do NOT be afraid because I am with you, I meant it. That's why I am with you now. What keeps you from experiencing me is you are focused on your suffering and what's happening with and around you.

- "Nothing will separate you from me, your Lord and your friend. Will anguish, or distress, or fear, or suffering? No, in all these things you are and will be more than conquerors because of my Love for you.

- "Neither death, nor life, nor angels, nor principalities, nor present things nor future things, nor powers, height nor depth, nor any other creature will be able to separate you from the Love of my Father and me."

St. Paul spoke these truths, not because he believed in them but experienced them and me.

- "We who are led by the Spirit are sons and daughters of God. You did not receive a spirit of slavery to fall back into fear, but received a spirit of adoption, because the God who created you is your Father and you are his son/daughter. If we are his children then you are his heir with Jesus."

- "So, join the suffering you are enduring with the sufferings of Jesus, for if you choose to suffer with

Jesus you will be glorified with him."

Jesus, _____ and I love you because you loved us first. We choose to continue trusting you to guide and walk through this with you no matter what happens or what lies ahead. Heal those things that will pass away and give us the faith, strength and courage to endure those that will not. AMEN!

CHAPTER 4
THE FAMILY GATHERS

FAMILY VISIT PRAYER WITH YOUR LOVED ONE

Jesus, it's good to be with you. We have come together as a family, to pray and ask you to heal and deliver us and _____ from our fears.

Help us to trust in you, and give everything to you now, so you can heal and deliver all of us from our fears.

Jesus, give us the grace to focus our attention on you, right here with us... (Pause 15 sec.) .

Lord, take all the negative thoughts, evil half-truths and lies that we have let into our minds, which are overwhelming us with worry and fear—fear that tempts us with doubt and even despair...take them right now, Lord. We give them to you...

Through the intercession of you, the Blessed Mother, St. Michael, and in the name of You, Jesus, our Lord and friend, deliver us from

- Fear, Doubt and Despair...   Bind and Cast them out
- Worrying about tomorrow   Bind and Cast them out
- Negative thoughts...   Bind and Cast them out
- Half Truths and Lies...   Bind and Cast them out

Instead, Jesus, we choose the **Truth**, that you are here with us. So give us the grace to not take any of these half-truths and lies back by thinking about or dwelling on them.

Replace our worrying about tomorrow and the future by staying in the present. (Pause 10 sec.)

Jesus, you said **love** dispels fear, so deliver our fears, not only with your love, but also our love for one another and all the people who love us.

_____, you are not alone. The Lord and we, your family, are with you.

(Place your hand on your loved one and pray)

HAIL MARY... Amen.

OUR FATHER... Amen.

(Trace the cross with your thumb on_____'s forehead, then express your love for one another verbally or an embrace.)

Enjoy your loved one and family and keep saying **'NO'** to the negative thoughts, half-truths and lies.

Stay in the present, aware that I am and will be with you whether you experience me or not. You are not alone and neither is your loved one.

CHAPTER 5
TOUGH DECISIONS AND LETTING GO

THE TOUGH DECISIONS BEFORE GRADUATION

JESUS:

If your loved ones body has died suddenly because of an accident, know that he/she has now left it and has been set free and is with family and friends who have already passed over and gone home.

If your loved one has struggled and suffered for a long or short period of time and has now entered into the last stages of their earthly life, by now you and your family will be called upon to make the most difficult choices you have ever made.

If your loved one has a 'Living Will', it will be easy to make those decisions, but it will still be a heavy, and I mean heavy burden, to instruct the doctor or caretaker to implement them. If they don't have a 'living Will' and you are the designated 'Health Care Proxy', then let me help walk you through them.

- Do not resuscitate

- Palliative care and Hospice

- Stop medication and feeding

- Remove Life Support

The minute you are faced with any of the above, in your mind, choose to say **'Lord'** and ask for my guidance, then remember, all of these decisions have absolutely nothing to do with you ending their life. You will be tempted to think so and may believe it, but this is Evil lying to you.

Say **NO** to it and remember the Truth that your loved one is not dying, only their physical body that is keeping them imprisoned in suffering and won't let go until you and your loved one succumb to fear, doubt, and despair.

You are experiencing what my Blessed Mother experienced when she watched me being scourged and crucified. She also heard my last words, crying out to my Father feeling alone and abandoned by him, but with my last breath I chose to let go of my body that was dying and focus on my Father who Loved me and entrusted my Spirit into His hands.

So, if your loved one has no 'Living Will' for their life ending wishes, and if they are unconscious or in a coma and you are the Health Care Proxy, spouse or next of kin to make the decisions, then remember this as you make the hard decisions, that you are not ending your loved ones life, but enabling them to leave their suffering behind, graduate, and begin their new and eternal life with me.

Finally, there will be no more suffering, pain, or death, and there are no human words to express the Peace, Joy, and Unconditional Love they will experience sharing in my resurrection.

Most of all, remember when you make these decisions keep reminding yourself that I am with you and this is the valley of darkness and shadow of death. You will be attacked by the most accusing lies; "you are killing your loved one; you are not helping them to stay alive longer; you are responsible for taking their life."

Remember, these are lies and will lay incredible guilt and fear on you. Resist them with faith and love.

Don't be afraid to make those decisions knowing that I will lead you from darkness to light, sadness to Joy, and from Fear to Love.

Once the decisions have been made, whether your loved one is alert, conscious, or unconscious, **tell them** what has been decided, and tell them that I am about to fulfill my promise to them, that they are and will be sharing in my resurrection and I will meet them when their body lets go of them. Tell them not to be afraid when it happens because they will experience a 'freedom' unlike anything they have ever known.

The degree to which they are afraid will be the degree to which they will struggle, but no matter what, when their body finally releases them, **I Will Be There**.

DEATH
A summary by Fr. Pompei

Dying is simply '**Letting Go**', which you have done from the beginning and throughout your whole life.

- Leaving Heaven where you (Your Consciousness, Mind, and Soul) were created, to be bonded with the Physical body your parents created and conceived here

- Leaving the swaddling comfort of your mother's womb at birth

- Leaving for kindergarten and school

- Leaving family, home, geography, friends, experiences, careers, activities that we enjoyed doing

- Letting go of your youth, parents, grandparents, spouses, siblings, health, and eventually your physical body

What makes letting go easier is Trusting in the Lord. There is that Verb again that by now, hopefully, Jesus has drilled into your mind and soul. It is what to do throughout your body's dying process.

So my Uncle Tony was right when he told me he wasn't afraid of dying and was at peace because he **Trusted** in the Lord his whole life.

"Francis, I only have to Trust Him one more time."

Now, that's the great reward of paying attention while you are here in school and listening to Jesus, your teacher.

ALLELUIA!

CHAPTER 6
DEATH: WHAT TO DO AND HOW TO DO IT

A PLAN FOR THE DEATH OF YOUR LOVE ONES BODY AND YOURS

This is probably one of, if not, the best gifts from Jesus to you—a Real Plan for your own death.

What? I am not kidding— a real plan to deliver you from the Fear of Your Death and your loved ones.

It is a step-by-step plan by Jesus Himself. Jesus not only has taught us about Suffering and Death, what to do about them, but also showed us how to do it.

He is going to teach you about your death and your loved ones; what thoughts you need to stop downloading that the world has burned into your mind. Then download His truth and dwell on them for the rest of your life and even on graduation day.

PHYSICAL DEATH: WHAT TO DO & HOW TO DO IT!

When your body enters into the process of dying, school is finally almost over. The suffering you or a loved one is enduring is final exams, and from what you have learned, it is the last time to **Trust** instead of succumbing to the negative thoughts, half- truths, and lies of Evil that are violently attacking and overwhelming you.

It is Satan's one last chance to steal your Spirit, light, and soul by tempting you to doubt God, despair and forsake

Him. Remembering what you learned about Satan, Evil, and how it works by putting thoughts and images in your mind, it will now be a final test of how much you have grown and practiced the steps to trust in the Lord.

If you have not spent your life working on your diploma of Trust that God sent you here to learn, then this will determine the degree that you will let fear, terror, panic, depression, doubt, and despair control your mind, emotions, and feelings.

Evil will convince you, as it has most people, that death is the end of you and your existence. It is here that you need to remember what Jesus taught you about Suffering and Death. They are not the real enemy when your physical body is ending. It is your Fear of them. That is what Jesus accomplished on the cross.

He refused to succumb to the temptation of Fear, the end of His life, and feelings of being abandoned by GOD (His Father). With His last words, He trusted by choosing to focus off the evil thoughts and lies in His mind. He focused His attention on His Father in Heaven as we all did when we were children and frightened and immediately focused off the pain and called for "Mommy." Remember?

<u>JESUS</u>:
"I was tempted by the thoughts and images of suffering that I would experience and succumb to Satan's power of Fear."

"Father, let this cup of suffering pass me by.

My fear turned into terror, and Satan threw me into agony and despair, so I cried out...

"Father, I beg you, let this cup of suffering pass me by"

Then I focused off the thoughts and images of Suffering and Death that I would experience the next day and even though Satan and Fear were still attacking me, I chose to pray to my Father and be given the strength and love to trust him anyway.

"Father, if this cup will not pass, and I must drink of it, then let it be done according to your will and not mine."

Finally, I found some peace in the midst of my suffering. The most important thing is my Father's and my unconditional love for you drove me to keep trusting and overcome my fear and despair."

"It is accomplished."

These attacks and temptations do not end once we trust. They can and will continue to attack many times more intensely. That is why when you are in the 'waiting rooms of life' in your doctor's office, or waiting for the condition of your loved one to change for the better even after you pray, you are still attacked, **RIGHT?**

However, the more you do the steps to **TRUST** and they become more natural to you, the easier it gets to train your mind to not download the evil thoughts, let go of them, and give them to the Lord. You may have to do this hundreds of times in the waiting rooms of life and continue to do it for the rest of your life until you graduate from school and leave your body.

Do not give up and do not surrender. When tempted, **Attack**, **Trust**, and then **Attack** some more.

Remember again what St. Paul said.

- "Our battle is not against flesh and blood, but the evil principalities, powers, and rulers of the Kingdom of Darkness in the Heavens." (Eph. 6:12)

What Jesus is teaching us is that trusting is the constant and the central action of our faith in Him and the Father.

The Truth is that there is a **War** going on in our bodies and in our minds. As I said before, it is a battle for our very soul, and the good news is that the Kingdom of God is now here. The Son of God, Jesus, our Lord and Savior, has won and given us the strength to endure our suffering, and He has given us the power and WILL to fight and resist Fear and Evil, as He did His.

A SUMMARY TEACHING:

Jesus has taught and told you what to do and shown you how to do it, so it is up to you to choose to not only believe it as the Truth and God's Will, but **DO IT!**

JESUS CONQUERS OUR FEAR OF DEATH

Jesus conquers Death by the **RESURRECTION**, His Transformation and the re-creation of His human body that was subject to Evil's Suffering and Death. What Jesus did by His Resurrection was create a renewed body, a perfect and divine physical body—YOURS, YOUR FUTURE, and **NOT** subject to suffering and Death.

JESUS:
"As I said to Martha, at the death of her brother and my close friend, Lazarus, I say to you now and ask you to listen very carefully.

I am the Resurrection and Life itself. If you believe and trust in me, when your physical body dies, I will raise you, your Spirit, Mind and Soul to live forever with me, with a re-created, perfect spiritual and physical body. My question to you, when your earthly body is dying, as it was to Martha, **Do you believe this?"**

NEUROSURGEON Dr. Eben Alexander
"I have spent decades, as a neurosurgeon and scientist, at some of the most prestigious medical institutions, but because of my coma and near death experience, I know beyond a doubt that our **Consciousness** lives on after our physical brains and bodies die. We are actually set free to a higher level of knowing, and that the universe is defined by an Unconditional Love for us. And that Unconditional Love is God."

Comment: Dr. Eben Alexander is a Harvard-trained neuro and brain surgeon who was an agnostic, but not anymore.

He had a near-death experience of God and Heaven. For more of his incredible story, his book is entitled Proof of Heaven. You can also find a wonderful convincing interview on YouTube. I highly recommend reading his story as he details his experience, not just of God and Heaven, but something that happened to him there that convinced him, without a doubt, that this all took place outside of his brain and physical body.

What convinced him was he met a young woman in heaven who welcomed and spoke to him. When he returned to his body and recovered, his teenage son had a school project to look up his ancestry. Eben helped his son because he knew it would be difficult. Eben was adopted at birth and didn't know his parents or if he had siblings.

After investigating he found that he did have siblings and met with them in a wonderful reunion. They told him he had another sister, but she died when she was young. When they showed him a picture of her, that's when Eben said, it was the most unbelievable experience he ever had in his entire life. It was the young woman who met him in heaven, which was the proof that his experience of going to heaven all took place outside of his brain and body. Read his story in his book, **Proof of Heaven**.

I included this story, because I not only believe it is true, but it represents a credible person, a Harvard trained brain and neuro- surgeon, an agnostic, who shows you the brain scans that reveal that the cortex was totally infected and non-functioning.

MY BROTHER LEFT HIS PHYSICAL BODY, GRADUATED, AND WE WERE THERE AND SAW IT

(My brother Fr. Fred Pompei, a Diocesan priest for 53 years graduated and left his body (School building) on April 11, 2019.)

The following is my sister Trish's account of what we experienced in the early hours that morning and the moment our brother left his body. My brother was a very Holy man and taught me, his little brother, how to follow Jesus and the Holy Spirit.)

It was no surprise that the Lord allowed him to be with Trish and me at his graduation and witness what he did to comfort us and 'Let Go'.)

These amazing things and signs were given to Francis and me as we stood by our wonderful brother in the hospital bed before he left this earth.

We gave glory to God for us arriving on time to be with him. He was not responsive and on life support when we got there. His eyes were closed and the women who loved him from the parish were there with him and all devastated. Francis and I grabbed his hand and spoke in his ear to tell him WE were there with him. He immediately opened his eyes and squeezed our hands. We were so heartbroken seeing him in the state he was in, but grateful he knew the 3 of us were all together.

As the night progressed and we had to make the decision to take off the life support which the Dr. agreed was the best option. We wiped his forehead with a damp warm cloth and held his hands. We told him over and over how much we loved him, and that he was the best brother we could ever want. Francis and I told him to start letting go and we would be ok......and would see him when we graduated.

Francis told him to keep looking for our Mom, Dad, St. Anthony, Blessed Mother and of course Jesus. When you see them, go where they tell you to go and do what they tell you to do. His eyes were closed and about an hour later in the wee hours of the morning, he all of a sudden started to move his mouth as if he was talking to someone.....there was no voice coming out of him, but he was definitely talking, moving his mouth as if in a deep conversation.

He then quickly lifted his right hand up in the air...and was pointing to someone, high above the ceiling......when he did that, he started waving real hard as if he saw and recognized someone and kept waving and waving excitedly. Francis and I knew he was actually seeing all the people who were coming to meet him at Heaven's door. We just knew it.....when he put his hand down from waving, his eyes were still closed.....

Francis and I grabbed each of his hands to hold them and he **suddenly and forcibly** pushed us away.... we couldn't believe it..... we knew he was telling us..... you already said goodbye....now it's time for me to go....... so as he always used to say to us...."leave me alone"... ha ha!

That's our brother Fred! Even though his earthly body was still shutting down, Francis and I knew without a doubt that's the moment he left his body and went to heaven when he pushed us away for the last time to tell us, "Time to let go."

We did with the heaviest of hearts and both felt we had lost part of our souls along with him, and even though we experienced these signs, it still hurts deeply not having him with us.

We are happy that Fred is out of pain and suffering. We will always miss him until we see him again when we graduate.

Thank you, Lord, for the love you gave to our wonderful brother.

Trish Pompei, (Fr. Fred's and Fr. Francis' sister)

Fr. Fred Pompei

CHAPTER 7
WHEN YOUR LOVED ONES BODY'S DEATH BEGINS

WHAT TO DO, THINK AND PRAY WHEN YOUR LOVED ONES BODY'S DEATH BEGINS

Do you remember having a graduation rehearsal the night before the big day, so you would know exactly what to do the next day? Well, here are the rehearsal details of what to do, what to pray, and how to think when your body is dying.

- As your senses quit functioning, things will start to dim. You may feel like you are in darkness like many who have had near death experiences feel they are in a tunnel.

- Don't be afraid and give in to lies, doubt and despair.

- Keep using your WILL to let go of your physical senses, and not try to make them function or be afraid they are not working.

- You will still be very aware of your Self, Consciousness, Mind, and Will. Using your WILL, choose to let go of your family, friends, and earthly life. This will be very difficult, but keep doing it, and keep reminding yourself what Jesus taught you. You will see them again when they pass over and graduate.

- Then focus off your body dying and look for Jesus and your loved ones who have already graduated.

- Keep talking to them and asking them to come for you. No matter how intense your feelings of fear, doubt, and despair may be, use your Will and keep choosing to look for Jesus and your loved ones until they come.

- Do so by repeating the words of Jesus on the cross when His body was dying.

"Into your hands, Lord, I commend my spirit."

- When you sense, see, or hear Jesus and your loved ones, do whatever they tell you to do, and go wherever they tell you to go.

- Don't be tempted to listen or go with anyone else, no matter how good it feels.

- Don't look back.

- *Even if your physical body and brain is in a coma, your Consciousness, Mind, and Soul will still be intact for you to follow the **Plan**, cross over, and **Graduate**.

Graduation Rehearsal is over. Now you know what to do and how to do it.

CHAPTER 8
GRADUATION: THE REAL 'PASSOVER'

FAMILY PRAYER SERVICE TO GUIDE YOUR LOVED ONE THROUGH GRADUATION TO ETERNAL LIFE

ORIENTATION

Spokes-person for family tells their loved one (Whether they are conscious or unconscious)

- Who is there

- What's happening medically and spiritually (According to Jesus)

Example:

"Dad, it's me Cathy your daughter, Joe is here and your grandchildren, Zach and Gabriela. We're here because we love you and don't want you to be alone.

Dad, what's happening is that you are in the hospital and there is nothing more that the doctors can do for your body which means that your body is dying and you should get ready to graduate and leave it.

We are all devastated to hear this and then have to tell you. We're all frightened and in the state of shock as you probably are now. (After you cry and embrace)

The good news, Dad, is that we all have faith and know that when your physical body ends, at that moment,

Jesus will raise you up and out of it and take you home to heaven where God created you.

Finally, you'll be free from all the suffering and fear your body has caused you.

So Dad, we want to pray together with you and ask Jesus to guide and lead us through your leaving and our letting you go.

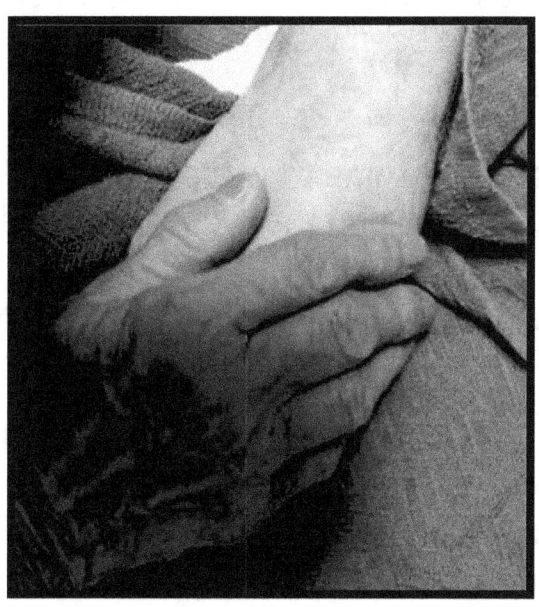

GRADUATION CEREMONY AND PRAYER

(Make a copy of this prayer for each member of your family. At this moment pass them out and then begin)

ALL PRAY:

In the name of the Father, Son, and Holy Spirit, Amen.

Lord, we are here together with you and our family and friends. Help us to be aware of you right here with us, because you have been waiting for us to acknowledge that you are.

Jesus, you said to "Come to you all who are laboring and heavy burdened and that you would give us rest."

_____ and we are heavy burdened and need to feel your presence and hear your words to lift us from sadness to hope.

Help us to "Be Still" and drop down from our thoughts and feelings into our hearts and very soul for the Holy Spirit, your unconditional Love, to fill this room and us. (Pause 10 seconds)

We love you Lord and it's good to be with you.

Negative and Evil thoughts are tempting us as they attacked you when your body was suffering and dying.

Tell us the Truth, Jesus, that will cast out the evil lies that

_____ 's life is ending.

(Go around and each person present be Jesus' voice to speak His words)

- "Peace be with you. It's me, Jesus, your Lord and most of all, your friend. I have heard your prayers and thank you for trusting me."

- "These are the moments that all of you have dreaded. You are experiencing what my blessed Mother did as she wept at the foot of my cross, watching suffering and death destroy my body.

- "The World and Satan will tell you that death is the end of your life, nevermore to exist. This is a **lie** and the reason I came, to destroy death once and for all, by raising you up from your physical body."

- "I am with you and have never left your side since you were born. If you are feeling alone and that I have abandoned you, so did I feel that way about my Father. In spite of my fear of the end of my life and feeling abandoned by my Father, I chose to **trust** him with my last breath.

- _____, join your suffering and feelings to mine and trust me as I trusted in my Father."

- I tell all of you this, "The sufferings that you are experiencing now are as nothing compared to the glory I will give to _____ and all of you when I raise you up."

- _____, your family and friends who are with me in heaven are more excited than you could ever imagine and waiting for your body to let you go and set you free. They already know what they will do when they see and embrace you. They are wondering what you will do and want you to start imagining and thinking about it.

- _____, the Father will dance with joy when you are finally 'Home'.

- So, stay the course.! Console yourselves with the Truth that I really am with and will be with you in the days to come.

ALL PRAY:

Thank you, Lord, for the gift of our faith. Without it we would despair and be without hope, but you are that hope and it is the hope of eternal life that there are no words to describe. We love you Lord and want to thank you.

Response: Thank you Lord...

- Jesus, for the gift of our faith... R. (All respond)

- For the Unconditional Love you had for us to endure your suffering and death... R.

- For your forgiveness of our sins and loving us anyway when we do... R.

- For your words that speak the truth... R.

- For you, yourself, being that truth... R.

- For the great gift of _____... R.

- For blessing our lives with _____... R.

- For all the wonderful memories, you, _____, have given us... R.

(Each can share their own thanksgiving to the Lord by saying,)

"Jesus, I want to thank you for...."

Letting go:
Family members, one at a time are invited to express to your loved one,

- Your Love

- That you will miss them until you see them again

- Not to worry about you and let Jesus take them home

- Look for _____ when you get there.

- Personal expressions of Your love

Guiding your loved one through what will happen:

(A family member or if you are alone, help your loved one to 'let go' by describing what will happen, what to think, pray, and who to look for.)

1. _____, your senses will dim and no longer function. When it happens focus on the Lord instead. Don't try to fix them, and most of all say **NO** to the **Fear** that will tempt you like it did Jesus

2. Look for Jesus, family members and your close friends who are already with the Lord.

3. Remember _____, _____. _____. etc.

   (All present describe to_____, whether they are conscious or not, **stories and memories** of the relationship they had with their family or close friends that you remember.)

4. When finished, say _____ , keep remembering and imagining them and asking Jesus, your family and friends that are with the Lord, to **come for you and take you home.**

5. **Keep doing this in your mind**. This will help you to focus on leaving your body and going to your real home where God created you, **finally**, **no more** suffering, no more pain, and no more death, only the unconditional love of God.

6. **When you see them**, do whatever they tell you and go wherever they take you, and don't look back or worry about us. We'll be fine and take care of one another.

7. **Don't stop for anything or anyone else**, just Jesus and your friends and family that you are now with.

8. **Until then, there's nothing to be afraid of**. Your family who loves you is right here with you, and we're not going anywhere. Just keep focused on the Lord until you graduate by saying with your mind what Jesus said when his body was ending,

"Father, into your hands I commend my spirit'.

9. _____, keep repeating it slowly every now and then until you see them.

END PRAYER:

ALL:
(Join hands around and with_____ or put hand on them, and **looking around at one another** pray),

HAIL MARY, full of grace, the Lord is with you. Blessed are you among women and blessed is the fruit of your womb, Jesus. Holy Mary, mother of God, pray for us sinners now and at the hour of our death, Amen!

OUR FATHER... **AMEN!**

(When you finish, one at a time, trace the cross with your thumb on your loved ones head, expressing your blessing and love.)

(After all finish, express your love for one another, verbally or with an embrace.)

LASTLY, whether your loved one is conscious or unconscious, share stories that you remember that the others may not have been part of.

Make sure you direct those stories not only to each other, but to your loved one whether they are conscious or in a coma. Trust me, they will hear and understand everything, but may not be able to respond because their physical body is no longer functioning.

The good news is this will continue to keep you and your loved one focused on your love with them and dispel not only your fear and sadness, but more importantly your loved ones. In addition to this they will experience they are not alone and surrounded by those who love them.

Keep telling stories and sharing with others who are there. Just hearing your voices and feeling your presence will be like seeing you stand and cheer for them as they start to cross the stage, get their diploma and graduate. (**Commence** their new and **Eternal Life**)

"THANK YOU JESUS!"

LEAVING THEM AFTER THEY HAVE PASSED

PRAYER

_____, it is so painful to look at your dead body, but we believe and know that you left it and Jesus raised you up and out of it. If you are still here in this room we love and miss you already.

Our only consolation is that you are no longer frightened and suffering. We hated seeing you that way and felt so powerless to help you and only wished we could take it away.

Jesus, grant us the grace to postpone our sadness and grief so that we can give _____ a great send off and celebrate the blessed gift of _____'s life to us, his family and friends.

_____, we really need you together with Jesus to help us through these next few days to make arrangements for others to thank God for your life and grieve with us. Help us to make those necessary decisions for a service and your resting place, decisions that I know will be very difficult.

Jesus as we leave _____'s body we are saying **'Lord'** as you taught us, so that we know that we are not leaving _____ alone because he/she is with you in heaven and through the Holy Spirit you are with us here. Amen.

CHAPTER 9
DEVASTATED AND SURREAL, BUT MUCH TO DO

FUNERAL ARRANGEMENTS

(For those who choose to have a viewing and cemetery service)

OBITUARY

Don't be burdened by what to say. You're just making your loved ones friends and the community know that she/he has graduated and where, when, and how they can express their sympathy and respects. Your funeral director will help you with all the arrangements.

CASKET or CREMATION URN

- As you move about picking out a Casket or Urn, you are not picking out furniture for your loved ones new home. They are already in their new home, Heaven.

- Every now and then say "**Lord**", and hear him whisper in your ear, "Remember, he/she is no longer in their body, and this casket or urn is only the receptacle for your loved ones body that they lived in.

- Choose whatever expresses your love for their physical body that you will miss and be thankful that they are no longer in it. Instead, imagine them set free by Jesus, from the suffering you had to observe they went through.

A PERSONAL STORY:

When my sister, Trish and I had to pick out a Casket for my brother, Fr. Fred, we did the above, prayed, and even asked our brother to help us. Forgive my language, but even though we prayed and asked our brother to help us pick out his casket, it "sucked" and seemed surreal. We both wept several times.

Then something wonderful and healing brought us from sadness to laughter.

We had bought our brother a 'My Pillow' for his birthday that we were going to celebrate when he returned in less than a week from Florida, but he graduated only a few days later and we weren't able to give it to him.

I was looking at the inside of a possible casket and the funeral director was explaining the cloth and then mentioned the lacing on the pillow.

The minute he said 'pillow' I'm convinced that my brother put this thought in my mind. So I called my sister over and said why don't we swap pillows and put the 'My Pillow" we got for Fred's birthday in his casket, then we can thank Jesus for his new spiritual body and we're taking care of his earthly body that he has left.

We began to cry and laugh at the same time and felt in some way He was behind the whole idea.

'Thank you Jesus for the gift of laughter.'

Having walked with thousands of people through the loss

of their loved one over 45 years of priesthood, I am convinced that the Lord allows our loved ones, after they graduate, to stick around and through little signs and non-coincidences let us know they are alive and well in heaven, finally free.

So, as you walk through these next few days, weeks, and months, keep your spiritual eyes and ears open to your loved ones desire to heal and console you.

THE FUNERAL SERVICE

(For those of you who have a church or private service at the Funeral Home.)

As Jesus said, "Do not let your heart be troubled." In other words, when you have to put together the Service wherever it is, **RELAX**. You will have plenty of help from the Funeral Director and your Minister. Here are some things to keep in mind when you do.

Have in your mind that you are celebrating your loved ones life and the gift from God that he/she was and is.

- Have in your mind that you are giving all those who knew and loved them the opportunity to not only remember and celebrate their life, but find consolation from the Lord, the Service, and all those attending.

- The Service is an opportunity to include close family members and friends of your loved one.

- You will, if you haven't already, be offered by many

people, "If there is anything I can do please let me know."

- Asking them to be Pall bearers, Readers, Eulogist, Music, Prayers of Petition, etc., will help them and you give your loved one a blessed and magnificent graduation and send- off. It will help console and heal all those who participate in _____ 's graduation ceremony.

JESUS:
"I just wanted to remind you as you are reading that I am still right here with you. Take 5 seconds and enjoy the peace of mind knowing that you're not alone and this will all work out. Thank you for trusting me from moment to moment. I'm proud of you and most of all I love you. So keep reading!

OPEN OR CLOSED CASKET
This is a choice for you and your family to make. For some you may not want to see your loved one lifeless in a casket. For others they may want to see them suffering no more, and see their earthly body for the last time.

Suggestion:
Share your feelings about when you saw them suffering and the images that are still overwhelming you.

The question is, do you want to see or have those who come to pay their last respects see their friend lifeless in a casket and have that be their last image of them, or you don't want your last memory of their body to be dead in a casket.

Be sensitive to each other's choice of what they cannot handle.

<u>Personal Choice</u>:

My sister and I had enough images to deal with watching my brother suffer and take his last breath. We decided to have a closed casket and did not view my brother's body after the funeral director prepared it. Instead, we had a wonderful picture-poster of him on an easel next to his casket.

We also chose not to go to the cemetery or have an internment service. We decided to visit his body at the cemetery when we felt ready.

When the service ended we all went to the reception and encouraged everyone to meet others who loved my brother and tell their stories, which proved to be very healing for everyone, sensing he was present in those stories.

Everyone commented how wonderful it was meeting and sharing stories about my brother and that they felt like we all gave him a great send-off and graduation party.

Ask the Lord to bless your conversation before you make the decision and trust him.

<u>EULOGY</u>

(For those of you who are asked to give the Eulogy)

In recent years, at least in the Catholic Church, pastors have or have not permitted a family member to give a eulogy.

There has been a trend in many churches to not have a eulogy. Instead, the family meets with their Pastor and shares important thoughts about their loved one that might be included in the sermon.

The main reason for not allowing a eulogy is that people don't know what it is and get carried away lasting too long.

Therefore, whoever gives the eulogy, make a copy of the following guidelines and what and what not to include in it, lasting 5 minutes, maximum. (You have my permission)

EULOGY GUIDELINES

A EULOGY: is your personal testimony to a few outstanding qualities of your loved ones life being celebrated.

- It should avoid inside jokes and stories that no one understands or was part of.

- It should be brief and to the point, no longer than 5 minutes. More than this may have a negative effect on those attending.

- If there is more than one person giving the eulogy, keep the 5 minute maximum, each person's remarks should be only 2 ½ minutes.

- If two are giving the eulogy, 1½ pages typed double spaced takes about two and a half minutes.

- If one person is giving the eulogy, 2 pages, or less, typed (double spaced) is about 5 minutes.

- The eulogist should encourage everyone to share their stories with one another after the service, at the cemetery, and the reception.

- For Eulogies that you want to be longer: Type it out, make copies, and have the ushers pass them out as people leave, or folded and placed in the program.

EULOGY CREATION FORM:

Use the following to help you outline and then type your eulogy.

Qualities:

1. _____
2. _____
3. _____

A Very Brief Story of of the 3 Qualities:

Story #1 _____
Story #2 _____
Story #3 _____

VIEWING YOUR LOVED ONES BODY IN THE CASKET

(Open or Not, or in an URN, if cremated)

This is one of the things that you have probably thought about many times and dreaded when it would actually happen.

Well, it's happening and all the thinking about it and trying to prepare for it just doesn't seem to help.

The Truth is that it will be so overwhelming and numbing and you haven't even gone to the Funeral Home.

So, what to do:
Just before you enter the room or wherever they have been placed, say your Trust word, "**Lord**".

Become aware that the Lord is right there with you, because he knows you really need him and need him now.

As you approach your loved ones body, imagine the Lord is walking right next to you, because he is.

JESUS:
When Martha came to me and told me that her brother, my good friend Lazarus was dead, I wept with her and her sister Mary.

Then I asked them where have you laid him, and **together**, **arm and arm**, we went to the tomb where they had placed my friend. I know what you are feeling and the depth of those horrific images of your loved ones body when you first see them.

I wept bitterly as probably you will and that is good. Your tears express as mine did, how much we love them. Tears are also a gift that I gave you when you were created. They are the way to release all your fears, sadness, grief, but also the expression of the greatness of your love.

As you look upon your loved one, listen to me whisper in your ear,

"This is the body that they lived in, but they are not dead. I have already raised them from their body and taken them to Heaven, but their very Spirit that you love, is closer than you think."

THE WAKE:

Some things to keep in mind at the Wake or viewing if you have one.

- You will meet people who you don't know, but loved _____.

- Think about postponing your grieving and help those people who come to heal their grief.

- By just talking to and embracing them, they will feel the presence of your loved one whom they are grieving their loss.

- Listen carefully to their stories of their relationship with and why they loved Him/Her. You will experience much healing from their stories as you learn things about your loved one that you didn't know.

A SHORT PRAYER BEFORE YOU LEAVE
(At the Casket or Urn Table)

LEADER:
Thank you Lord and for being with us to get us through this wake service.

And thank you _____ for all the wonderful people who loved and will miss you.

Jesus, heal them in the days to come as you heal us.

We Love you _____ and we miss you so much already.

We want to really celebrate your life and give you a great send off at the funeral service.

Join us now from Heaven _____, as together we pray,

HAIL MARY...   **Amen.**
OUR FATHER...   **Amen**.

In the name of the Father, Son, and Holy Spirit, Amen.

(You might want to embrace one another before you leave)

THE NIGHT BEFORE THE FUNERAL SERVICE

By now you are exhausted and numb, tired of preparations, calling and talking to people.

You're normal!

You probably haven't gotten any sleep in a couple days or more. Be good to yourself is what the Lord wants you to do.

From the time you got the phone call until now, you need to find times (more than one) to let go of all the things you had and have to do. Go to your bedroom, get away from everyone and everything, and try to get some sleep.

If you can't, just close your eyes and hear the Lord whisper in your ear,

"Don't answer the door or phone, rest, just rest."

Try to find these sacred moments every day to get away with the Lord, not to pray, but simply rest.

CHAPTER 10
VISITING THE CEMETERY

PRAYER

LORD, BLESS THIS RESTING PLACE FOR _____'S EARTHLY BODY

Let us pray:

In the name of the Father, Son, and the Holy Spirit, Amen.

Lord, just as you wept at the site of your friend Lazarus's tomb, we too are overwhelmed with grief at the sight of _____'s grave.

We miss _____ beyond words. That's why we are here as his/her family and turn to you for healing and deliverance from the awful thoughts and images of his physical body dying and now in this grave.

Jesus, we have gathered here as_____'s family to experience our love for one another and _____.

Give us the grace to focus off the end of his/her earthly life and instead focus on you right here with us.

Lift us up from sadness to Joy with the knowledge that we were blessed to have_____ as a gift from you.

Lord, speak to us the Truth and give us the faith to believe that _____ is not dead but with you in heaven.

Reader:

"I am the resurrection and Life itself, when your earthly body dies, I will raise you up and out of it, like _____'s

Remember this Truth when you are attacked by Satan and Evil's lies. Your earthly life is school and the death of your bodies is 'graduation' and 'commencement' of your new life.

Learn to believe and trust me that the sufferings you are experiencing now are nothing compared to the glory I will manifest in you as I have in_____.

Call to mind and remember often, I love you, always have and always will."

PETITIONS: **Response: Thank you, Jesus**

- Lord, thank you for the great gift of _____

- Jesus, thank you for your resurrection that _____ is sharing in… R.

- Thank you for helping_____and us to overcome our fear of suffering and death… R.

- Give us the strength to let go of _____ and enjoy his/her new life in heaven… R.

- Grant _____ to experience freedom from all the pain and suffering from his/her earthly life… R.

- You said that the sufferings of the present are as nothing compared to the glory you will manifest in us when we leave our earthly bodies. May _____'s glory be great in heaven, with no more tears, suffering and death… R.

- In the days to come, Lord, heal our hearts and minds with the knowledge that we will see her/him again when we graduate, and on that day there will not only be no more death, but no more separation from our loved ones like there is now… R.

_____, we will continue to pray and talk to you and be open to signs and awareness that you are not far away… R.

(A family member reads the following from your loved one)

"IT'S ME, _____

YOU PICTURE DEATH AS COMING TO DESTROY ME;
Picture instead Jesus took me to my real home, in heaven, where God created me.

YOU THINK OF DEATH AS MY LIFE ENDING;
Think of my new life as beginning and there are no words to describe what I am experiencing.

YOU THINK OF MY GOING AS A LOSS;
Think instead of what I have found; freedom from fear, suffering and Death.

YOU THINK OF ME AS PARTING FROM YOU;
Think rather that I have graduated and met God, who has always unconditionally loved me, and all the people I loved and love me who are already here with me.

YOU THINK OF ME AS LEAVING;
Think of me as arriving in heaven, because I have, and the Joy and Love I'm experiencing is greater than anything I could have imagined like Jesus said."

SO, WHEN THE VOICE OF DEATH WHISPERS TO YOU, "YOU ARE DYING AND YOUR LIFE IS ENDING"; Hear Jesus' voice and mine saying,

"You are graduating from your body and coming home with me, to be together forever." It's all **True**! I love you and will be waiting. Keep talking to me, because I'm not far from you and only your physical body separates us.

BLESSING OF YOUR LOVED ONES RESTING PLACE

Lord, we bless the resting place of _____'s earthly body. Through Your resurrection, we believe and know that he is not here, but with you. On the last day you will recreate a perfect body like yours for _____ and us, and there will be no more pain, suffering, and death; only the memories of our experiences of love for one another.

_____, until we are all once again together forever, we bless your body's resting place and make it holy by the Love of Jesus and ours, your family. Amen!

(When Holy Water is available all sprinkle and bless the resting place. If no Holy Water pray the following)

HAIL MARY… Amen

OUR FATHER… Amen.

FINAL PRAYER:

As we go our separate ways_____, we will

miss you terribly and console each other with the knowledge that we will see you again when we graduate.

We promise to heal one another with the many funny and wonderful stories and memories you have given us. We love you _____, Amen.

(If you remain, continue to share stories about your loved one and make sure you keep in mind while you are telling them that your loved one is closer than you think.)

CHAPTER 11
WHEN EVERY ONE GOES HOME

WHEN EVERYONE GOES HOME, AND YOU TO AN EMPTY HOUSE

There is nothing you can do to prepare you for this moment. Knowing what may or will happen might help you to cry out to the Lord again to be with you before you set foot in yours or your loved ones home.

I dreaded going back to where I lived, knowing that it was only me and the preparation, wake and service were over, and the people gone. The loneliness and void was like getting hit with a train.

Everything I looked at or touched that was related to my brother reminded me that he was no longer home or in the hospital. He would no longer come visit me and watch a game in his favorite chair, and his large cup of ice water that would never be used again.

I just sat, stared at the wall as the spiritual and mental Novocain wore off. Then the realization that my brother's body was gone and so was he, and I would never see him ever again for the rest of my life.

After I stopped crying, I said, "Lord, this sucks and I have a physical pain in my chest. Is this what it means to have a broken-heart? If it is, I have it."

By talking to the Lord, I stopped focusing on the pain and started being aware of the Lord with me. Then I started talking to my brother as if he was right there too, as he had been many times before.

I told him how awful this experience was and missed him with no words to describe how it feels.

Then I continued talking about all the things that my sister and I had to do and all the wonderful people and his friends who he had told us about but we never met, friends who loved him very much.

I told him all the stories people told me about him that I never knew. It was like he had a whole other life and never knew so many wonderful ways he touched other people.

The more I talked to him the more I sensed he was truly alive, with the Lord and happy. Even though I missed him beyond words, I was taking my first steps to grieving and learning how to live life that is and will now be different until I see him again when I graduate.

I offer this as a way to deal with going home alone when the service is over and all the people have gone. Later, I have included a chapter on 'Grieving' that I hope will really help you.

CHAPTER 12
CLEANING THEIR ROOM AND BELONGINGS

When it is finally over and you have to go home to an empty house, you will get hit like an 18 wheeler truck with the reality of the emptiness, void, and the incredible loss and loneliness. Add to that the thought that it will never be the same intensifies all the feelings and emotions and tempts you maybe with anger, depression and despair. Everything you see of their belongings and your own pictures of them screams out at you that they are gone forever.

If you are experiencing this, you are **Normal**.

As you browse around you will learn a great deal about them you didn't know and things that you remembered and loved about them. You will both be saddened and smile at the memories that will go through your mind. As painful as this is, I believe it is the beginning of your grieving and dealing with **'that life is and will be different."**

Given this, now would be a great time to STOP what you are doing and say, **"Lord".** Focus off all your feelings and emotions and choose to ask the Lord to be aware that he is right there with you. Tell him how much this is an overwhelming task and to keep you aware that he is with you and that your loved one is with him and not far away.

You might even talk to them as you would if they were really there going through their "personal belongings'. It may just help your faith to believe this, but actually experience their presence and the Lord's.

My last and strong suggestion is to bring family or close

friends with you to help decide what to keep and what to give away. You can't beat the love and support of your family and friends' presence. Isn't that what family and friends are for, to laugh and to cry with you and help lift you from your feelings of being alone to do this.

A PRAYER FOR YOU AND THOSE WITH YOU BEFORE YOU BEGIN CLEANING THEIR ROOM

In the name of the Father, Jesus our Lord and friend, and the Holy Spirit, the Comforter, Amen.

Lord, this is a task that we have dreaded to do, so we are asking that we start by choosing to be aware that you are with us, because you said you would be.

As we go through belongings from _____ 's earthly life, give us the knowledge and grace that they are **Not** dead but are with you and they are not far from us, separated only by our physical bodies.

_____, it's your family and friends. As we go through your belongings, put memories in our minds that will reveal your love for us and your desire to heal our sadness.

If and when we cry and feel sad we want you to know it's because we miss and love you.

So _____, together with you we pray to you Father, in the words Jesus taught us to pray with.

'OUR FATHER…. Amen.

CHAPTER 13
NO FAMILY AND NO ONE TO REMEMBER

- What if you are alone and there is no one to be with your loved one who is suffering or ready to graduate?

or

- When you know someone who has no family or friends who is suffering and may be dying

As a Franciscan Friar, I have spent much of my time living and working with the poor. Eleven of those years I spent at St. Francis Inn, Philadelphia, a soup kitchen, Women's Center, Thrift Store, and shelter. It was in one of the worst neighborhoods in the United States. We fed 350 to 400 people twice a day all year long.

Many of our senior guests, homeless individuals, and families lived in abandoned buildings. Because many were living alone without any family, we became their family. When they died there was absolutely no one to make any kind of arrangements for their death, funeral, services and interment.

I became very aware of those throughout the world who had no one to help support them and be with them, especially children, who lost their entire families from

- Earthquakes
- Tornados
- Tsunami
- War
- Violence

They are not exempt from the trauma that this book has described at the loss of their loved one. There is no one to celebrate or remember their lives, ignored by the rest of society, letting the local government or in many poor countries, neighbors or strangers to bury them.

At the St. Francis Inn when I was there, and I know that they are still doing it, we took care of all the arrangements, provided a casket and cemetery plot. More importantly, we transformed the soup kitchen into a funeral parlor, had a wake service, funeral service, and invited all our guests to attend as well as our community of friars, sisters, lay volunteers, and young Franciscan Volunteers.

My intention and hope here is to make all readers aware that there is another world out there where children to seniors are used, abused, tortured, traumatized and murdered. They have never experienced love or family, only hatred, violence, filled with fear, loneliness, and hopelessness.

I strongly encourage you who are reading this book and lost a loved one, to seek out locally any private or public program that deals with those who have died without anyone to acknowledge and celebrate their life.

On a personal note, the services that we had at St. Francis Inn for those who had no family were some of the most wonderful moments to experience God's presence there with us and his unconditional love for **all** of us, especially those who have no one, that we are all precious to the Lord. Because we chose to acknowledge their lives we felt God's love for us.

A PRAYER SERVICE FOR THOSE WHO HAVE NO ONE TO REMEMBER THEIR LOVED ONE WITH

Jesus, My heart is broken and I feel so lost and alone. There is no one else here to remember _____, no family and no friends.

I feel like I am all alone in the universe. That's why I am praying to you God, _____'s creator and mine. I need your help to guide me in what to do, to not only remember them but let them know what a precious gift they were and are to not only me, but to you.

Be merciful to them Lord. Forgive their weaknesses and sins.

Heal all the pain and suffering they experienced in their earthly life. Welcome them to Heaven and grant them what you said would be awaiting them and all of us who believe and love you.

- "The sufferings of the present are as nothing compared to the glory I will manifest in you."

- "In my Father's house there are many mansions."

- "Come, blessed of my Father, and inherit the kingdom prepared for you from the beginning of time."

- "I am the resurrection and the life. Anyone who believes in me, when their earthly physical body dies, I will raise them up and take them to heaven where I created them, their real home."

- "Do not be afraid or let your hearts be troubled. I am with you and will be until the end of time."

"Remember that I love you and that you will see your loved one again when you graduate and come home. We will all be together, no more suffering, death, and no more separation from one another forever.

Celebrate your loved ones' life by following me and loving others as you loved _____."

"You are not alone. I am with you. All you need to do is say "**LORD**", close your eyes, be still, and imagine I am there with you, **because I am**."

CHAPTER 14
GRIEVING

Grief is a natural response to loss. It's the emotional suffering you feel when something or someone you love is taken away. Often, the pain of loss can feel overwhelming.

You may experience all kinds of difficult and unexpected emotions, from shock or anger to disbelief, guilt, and profound sadness. The pain of grief can also disrupt your physical health, making it difficult to sleep, eat, or even think straight. These are normal reactions to loss—and the more significant the loss, the more intense your grief will be.

Coping with the loss of someone or something you love is one of life's biggest challenges. You may associate grieving with the death of a loved one—which is often the cause of the most intense type of grief—but any loss can cause grief, including:

- Divorce or relationship breakup
- Loss of health
- Losing a job
- Loss of financial stability
- A miscarriage
- Retirement
- Death of a cherished pet
- A loved one's serious illness

- Loss of a friendship
- Loss of safety after a trauma
- Selling the family home

Even subtle losses in life can trigger a sense of grief. For example, you might grieve after moving away from home, graduating from college, or changing jobs. Whatever your loss, it's personal to you, so don't feel ashamed about how you feel, or believe that it's somehow only appropriate to grieve for certain things. If the person, animal, relationship, or situation was significant to you, it's normal to grieve the loss you're experiencing.

Whatever the cause of your grief, though, there are healthy ways to cope with the pain that, in time, can ease your sadness and help you come to terms with your loss, find new meaning, and eventually move on with your life.

The grieving process
Grieving is a highly individual experience; there's no right or wrong way to grieve. How you grieve depends on many factors, including your personality and coping style, your life experience, your faith, and how significant the loss was to you.

Inevitably, the grieving process takes time. Healing happens gradually; it can't be forced or hurried—and **there is no "normal" timetable for grieving**. Some people start to feel better in weeks or months. For others, the grieving process is measured in years. Whatever your grief experience, it's important to be patient with yourself and allow the process to naturally unfold.

MYTHS AND FACTS ABOUT GRIEF AND GRIEVING
www.heartachetohealing.com

Myth: The pain will go away faster if you ignore it.
Fact: Trying to ignore your pain or keep it from surfacing will only make it worse in the long run. For real healing, actively deal with it.

Myth: It's more important to "be strong" in the face of loss.
Fact: Feeling sad, frightened, or lonely is a normal reaction to loss. Crying doesn't mean you are weak. Showing your true feelings can help you.

Myth: If you don't cry, it means you aren't sorry about the loss.
Fact: Crying is a normal response to sadness, but it's not the only one. Those who don't cry may feel the pain just as much and have other ways of showing it.

Myth: Grieving should last about a year.
Fact: There is no specific time frame for grieving. How long it takes differs from person to person.

Myth: Moving on with your life means forgetting about your loss.
Fact: Moving on means you've accepted your loss- but that's not the same as forgetting. You can move on with your life and keep the memory of someone or something you lost as an important part of you. In fact, as we move through life, these memories can become more and more integral to defining the people we are.

HOW TO DEAL WITH THE GRIEVING PROCESS

While grieving a loss is an inevitable part of life, there are ways to help cope with the pain, come to terms with your grief, and eventually, find a way to pick up the pieces and move on with your life.

- Acknowledge your pain.

- Accept that grief can trigger many different and unexpected emotions.

- Understand that your grieving process will be unique to you.

- Seek out face-to-face support from people who care about you.

- Support yourself emotionally by taking care of yourself physically.

- Recognize the difference between grief and depression.

We might think of the grieving process as a roller coaster, full of ups and downs, highs and lows. Like many roller coasters, the ride tends to be rougher in the beginning.

The difficult periods should become less intense and shorter as time goes by, but it takes time to work through a loss. Even years after a loss, especially at special events such as a family wedding or the birth of a child, we may still experience a strong sense of grief.

HOW TO GRIEVE THE LOSS OF YOUR LOVED ONE
Trish Pompei and David Watson

TRISH POMPEI:

We always think we prepare for the death of a loved one and know that perhaps time will heal the pain... well it doesn't... the pain, emptiness and hole in your heart will always be there. Life does go on but it's different... and that's the thing one has to learn to adjust to. Since my brother Fred 'graduated', there hasn't been a day that has gone by that I don't cry, even if only for a second.

When those thoughts come back to me of the day he took his last breath while my brother Francis and I were at his bedside is when my emotions get the best of me. I still feel that awful moment that seems surreal.

I have learned that when these terrible memories enter my mind, I ask Jesus and my brother Fred to help me concentrate on positive ones and more importantly that this was the moment that Jesus took his hand and walked him through Heaven's Door. I immediately say out loud and talk to Fred and tell him that I'm sad today because I can't see you in person, but I know you are happy in Heaven and that makes me happy.

Then I picture him with my parents, relatives and all the friends that are there with him celebrating, laughing and feeling whole again. Each day I try to do a small act of kindness for somebody and say "This is for you Fred".

I also wear the cross he wore around his neck as a Priest so I can feel that he is with me throughout the day. This all might sound silly, but that's how I deal with missing him. Do I have to do this every day... YES!

Does it make my heart feel less empty... no it doesn't, but it does give me solace to know that my brother isn't suffering anymore and does not have any bad days here on earth, only happy ones for eternity until I see him again when I graduate.

DAVID WATSON:
(A young man took my daughter's life. Jenni was only 20)

Dealing with Such a Devastating Loss

I found myself finding and reading passages, quotes, etc. to somehow learn how to survive this. Like below:

"Her smile and heart will always shine through
with such gratitude and such pride.
When we say your name you haven't died.
Every day in so many ways you are still with us
Time slips by but memories stay
Always in thought, and in heart.

We hold you close within our hearts
And there you will remain,
To walk with us throughout our lives

And the sweetness of her memory time can neither dim nor end.
We keep alive your memory everyday living as you did with passion, joy, faith, courage, strength, love and dedication to each other."

I quickly found that grieving has no playbook, there is never closure, it never ends, it becomes part of you and your everyday living, it is highly personal and at times very lonely. I found that Jenni-Lyn lives on when we dare to let ourselves remember. That the memories do cause pain, tears and deep emotions but truly are a blessing. I recall them as often as I wish---knowing a happy memory never wears out. They are a gift from Jenni-Lyn, I keep them close to my heart, and let these memories along with love, faith and hope be my sustaining power during these trying days.

Along this path of discovery, I found myself not only teaching myself how to grieve, I was also teaching others. Without knowing it my first lesson was given to a friend of Jenni-Lyn's in the receiving line at her calling hours. Jenni-Lyn's friend had a look on her face and she said to me "I don't know what to say." I immediately said to her in all seriousness "This sucks, doesn't it?" She later wrote to us and said how much that helped her be able to sort out her feelings, remember, and cherish her memories of Jenni-Lyn.

Some quotes that have helped me are:

From Winnie the Pooh – "You're braver than you believe, and stronger than you seem and smarter than you think"

From Helen Keller "What we once enjoyed we can never lose. All that we love deeply becomes a part of us"

From Abraham Lincoln - "And in the end it's not the years in your life that count. It's the life in your years"

The grief ebbs and flows, the heartache, the emptiness —it never goes away. It doesn't feel like 10 years. Feels more like yesterday, the emptiness is always there. I live each day with a pain no parent should ever have to endure.

However, **the celebration of a life** is way more important, and we try to do that every single year — every day of the year. I wish Jenni-Lyn was still with us on earth, but I also believe Jenni-Lyn lived exactly as she wanted to.

FR. FRANCIS POMPEI OFM

The truth is for me and my sister that missing our brother, life will never get 'better', but will only be 'different'. Those of you who are reading this, who loved your loved ones, will miss them for the rest of your lives until you graduate and see them again. What do you think?

TWO GREAT GIFTS FROM GOD FOR HEALING
Fr. Francis Pompei ofm

Now that I am an "old goat" and ministered to thousands of people for 45 years, I have learned that the Lord gave all of us two incredible Gifts to deal with Suffering and Life. Both of these need to be developed and experienced.

One gift has the power of God to deliver us from fear, worry, anger, grief, sadness, depression, and even despair. The other helps put all of our problems and suffering that overwhelm us into perspective and lifts us out of them to a 'freedom zone' of elation and joy, which we thought was impossible. What are these two wonderful gifts that the Lord has given us?

TEARS & LAUGHTER

TEARS, CRYING, EVEN WAILING will turn into a volcano eruption, finally releasing the pressure and darkness of Fear, Worry, Stress, Loneliness. When we stop crying, there is peace and rest. The flames of suffering cool down until they build up again. But we remain in gratitude for peace to come.

LAUGHTER, I mean a good belly laugh, when you feel like your chest is going to explode, and you can't stop. I hope you have experienced at least one. If you have had the laugh in the middle of a disaster, or a really, really BAD day, then you know what I mean.

Laughter lifts us up from the temptation of despair and thinking that it can't get any worse. Laughter at that moment catapults us magically and miraculously into another zone filled with joy, elation, and hope. When we finally stop laughing, we receive the truth and realization that it's not **the end of the world**. As the Lord and the Word of God says, **"It came to pass."**

On a personal note, I'm convinced laughing is reality, and **not** the unreality of problems, stress and suffering that seem to be permanent but will ultimately pass.

LAUGHTER IS A TASTE OF "HEAVEN"

JESUS:

LET ME CONSOLE YOU WITH THE TRUTH

"Heaven and Earth will pass away, but my words will never pass away."

I myself am the Truth, the Way, and the Life. My words and my unconditional love for you will dispel your fear and sadness with **Hope** that casts out evil's lies

> **Read what you believe.**
> **Believe what you read.**
> **Trust what you believe.**

#1
"Brothers and sisters:
Behold, I tell you a mystery. We shall not all fall asleep, but we will all be changed in an instant, in the blink of an eye, at the last trumpet, for the trumpet will sound, the dead will be raised incorruptible and we shall all be changed. For that which is corruptible must clothe itself with incorruptibility and that which is mortal must clothe itself with immortality. Then the word that is written shall come about:

> 'Death is swallowed up in victory. Where, O Death, is your victory? Where, O Death, is your sting?'

Thanks be to God who gives us the victory through

our Lord Jesus Christ." (1 Cor. 15: 51-57)

#2
"We do not want you to be unaware, brothers and sisters, about those who have fallen asleep, so that you may not grieve like the rest, who have no hope.

For if we believe that Jesus died and rose, so too will God, through Jesus, bring with him those who have fallen asleep.

Indeed, we tell you this, on the word of the Lord, that we who are alive, who are left until the coming of the Lord, will surely not precede those who have fallen asleep." (I Thess. 4:13-18)

#3
"Brothers and sisters,
Our citizenship is in heaven and from it we also await our savior, the Lord Jesus Christ. He will change our lowly body to conform with his glorified Body by the power that enables him also to bring all things into subjection to himself." (Phil. 3:20-21)

#4
"Brothers and Sisters,
We know that if our earthly body, a tent should be destroyed, we have a building from God, a dwelling not made with hands, eternal in heaven. And so, we are always courageous, although we know that while we are in these earthly bodies we are away from the Lord, for we walk and live by Faith, not by what we see."
(2 Cor. 5: 6-10)

#5

"Therefore, we are not discouraged rather, although our outer self is wasting away, our inner self is being strengthened and renewed day by day. For this momentary suffering that will pass away is producing for us an eternal glory that is beyond all comparison."
(Cor. 4:14)

JESUS:

I want you to not only believe in my Words and Truth, but to experience them.

So, close your eyes, use your imagination, and picture your loved one/s who are already here with me. As those images appear to you, they are from your loved one whose love for you has never ceased but has been perfected.

So, Just **'Be'** and enjoy their presence.

When you finish, I want you to imagine what both they and you will do when you graduate and see them again. As you do it, let your imagination explode with Joy and Love that no human words could ever capture.

And, as you embrace each other again, rejoice in knowing that there will not only be no more suffering and death, but **no more separation** from them for all eternity.

Then, as the scripture says,

"The Father and I will Dance"

CHAPTER 15
WHAT WILL HEAVEN BE LIKE?
Frequently asked questions about eternity.
Peter Kreeft

Why won't we be bored in Heaven?

I suspect this question subconsciously bothers most of us more than we like to admit. I can remember having something of a crisis of faith as a child: I thought I didn't want to go to Heaven since the popular pictures of it seemed pretty boring to me.

We will complete the very love-works we are meant to do on Earth. There are only six things that never get boring on Earth, six things that never come to an end: knowing and loving yourself, your neighbor, and God. Since persons are subjects and not objects, they are not exhaustible; they are like magic cows that give fresh milk forever.

The two great commandments that are our job description for life, in both this world and the next, express this plan: We must love God wholly and we must love our neighbor as ourselves. This never gets boring, even on Earth: getting to know and love more and more someone we already know and love. It is our clue and our preparation for our eternal destiny of infinite fascination.

Will we recognize our loved ones in Heaven?

Of course we will know our loved ones. This is a divinely designed, essential part of our joy. We are not designed to be solitary mystics, lovers of God alone, but to be, like God himself, lovers of men and women as well.

Just as Jesus on Earth loved each person differently and specially—he did not love John as he loved Peter, because John was not Peter—so we are designed to love people specially. There is no reason why this specialness should be removed, rather than added to, in eternity. Our family and special friends will always be our family and special friends.

In this life a child begins to learn to love by loving mother, then father, then siblings, then pets. The concentric circles of love are then gradually expanded, but the beginning lessons are never abandoned. There is no reason to think God rips up this plan after death.

How can I be happy in Heaven if someone I loved deeply on Earth doesn't make it to Heaven?

This brings up all sorts of other questions about emotions, relationships, and suffering in Heaven. These will be dealt with shortly, but the simplest and most important answer to this question for now is this: If there is someone you love and identify with so deeply that you cannot imagine being happy in eternity without him or her, and that someone seems now to be in peril of being unsaved, then use the relationship that God's providence has ordained for you.

Tell God that he has to arrange for this person's salvation as he has arranged for yours, because this person is a real part of you and for you as a whole to be saved, this person has to come along, just as your own body and emotions to come along. It need not be a "wheedling" or "blackmail" prayer; it can be a simple presentation of the facts, like Mary's "They have no more wine." Let God do his thing; it is always more loving, more gracious, and more effective than our thing, more than we can ever imagine or desire.

Can suicides be saved?
Yes. Most people who commit suicide are not in full control of their reason and thus are not fully responsible.
Suicide is a dreadful mistake, of course, and a terrible sin. Only un-repented sin locks Heaven's door, and sometimes sins are repented of at the same time they are committed, or immediately afterward.

The deeper part of a suicide's soul and will may believe and hope in and love God even while the surface part drives him to despair. Or repentance may come in an instant between the act and its result, death, or even *at* the moment of death. We do not know. Only God sees and judges hearts, not just acts, and God will use every possible means to save us.

Will we have emotions in Heaven?
I strongly suspect that we will have emotions in Heaven, for they are part of God's design for our humanity, and not only a result of the Fall. But our emotions will not drive us or control us. They will be no less passionate, but they will be less passive. Thomas Aquinas opines that sexual enjoyment was greater, not less, before the Fall (since sin always harms, never helps, every good thing), and Augustine opines that in Heaven the joy that we receive from God in our souls will "overflow" into our resurrection bodies in a "voluptuous torrent" of pleasure.

If we have emotions in Heaven, why won't we be sad about those we loved who are in hell?

We know there is no sadness in Heaven: God "will wipe away every tear from their eyes" (Rev. 7:17). I think we will not be sad about the damned for the same reason God is not. According to the Sermon on the Mount, he will say to them, "I never knew you" (Matt. 7:23). God will wipe our memories clean.

This is not falsehood or ignorance, but truth, for in a sense, the damned no longer are—that is, they no longer are in the most real place of all, Heaven. They no longer count. They are like ashes, not like wood. They once were fully human, fully alive, real men and women. But hell is a place not of eternal life but of eternal death. We do not love or weep over ashes; we only love or weep over the thing that existed before it was burnt.

In Heaven, however, we will not live in the past—we will have no regrets; nor will we live in the future—we will have no fears; but like God, we will live in the eternal present. Our heavenly emotions will be appropriate to present reality, not past reality.

Does this mean hell is unreal?

Certainly not, Jesus is very clear about the reality of hell. But he is also clear that it is death, not life, for the soul. In Greek philosophy, souls cannot die. In Christianity, they can—in hell. Is this annihilation? No, it is death.

Annihilation is the opposite of creation; death is the opposite of life.

What happens in hell?
Nothing

What happens in Heaven?
Everything

Can the blessed in Heaven see us now?
Let me put it this way: Is there any compelling reason why they shouldn't? Would their perfection be threatened thereby? Can Heaven be Heaven only by being quarantined and having the blinds drawn? It is reasonable to interpret the "cloud of witnesses" in Hebrews 12:1 not only as witnesses to their faith during their own lifetimes but as witnesses to us now.

Is there anything wrong with your love of your family? Will there be anything wrong with it in Heaven? Will there be anything wrong with your desire to see how they fare on Earth? I see no compelling reason to answer no.

Will we know everything in Heaven?
I think not. Only God is omniscient. We will never stop learning, but we will never come to the end, either. Only God can endure knowing everything without being bored.

Will we all be equal in Heaven?
We will be as we are now: equal in worth and dignity,

equal in being loved by God. But will we be equal in the sense of the same? God forbid! One of the chief pleasures of this life, as of the next, is the mutual sharing of different excellences, the pleasure of looking up to someone who is better than we are at something and learning from him or her.

The resentment expressed in saying, "I'm just as good as you are" is hellish, not heavenly. (By the way, that is one sentence that always means the opposite of what it says. No one who says it believes it.)

Do differences include sexual differences? Is there sex in Heaven?

Of course, sex is part of our divinely designed humanity. It is transformed, not removed, in Heaven. We will be "like the angels, neither marrying nor being given in marriage," according to Christ's answer to the Sadducees (Matt.22:30), but **not in being neutered**. Sex is first of all something we are, not something we do. I do not think we will be copulating in Heaven, but we will be busy being ourselves, and that includes being men and women, not genderless geldings.

What kind of bodies will we have in Heaven?

Christians say we will have transformed bodies, but real, physical bodies, as Christ had after his resurrection. His body could be touched and could eat. Yet it could come and go as he pleased, with neither walls nor distance as an obstacle. It was the same body he had before he died, and it was recognized as such by his friends. Yet it was so different that at first they did *not* recognize him.
I think our new resurrection body will be related to the body we have now in the same way that our current

body is related to the body we had in our mothers' wombs. If a fetus saw a picture of itself at the age of twenty, it would at first not recognize itself, so unforeseen and surprisingly new would it be. Yet it is the same self, even the same body, now grown radically more mature.

What of injuries and deformities? Will they all be removed in the resurrection body?

I think not. Christ still had his wounds. But they were badges of glory, not suffering and sadness. I think everything—in the body, in the soul, and in the person's world—that was offered to God and taken up into the eternal kingdom will be preserved and transformed and glorified in Heaven: but everything that was not— everything that was not the work of God or of the sanctified soul but was of the world, the flesh, or the devil—will be left outside Heaven's gate.

The martyrs' wounds will glow like gold, but the amputee's limb will be restored, and so will the brain-damaged person's intelligence. God's justice and mercy are perfect, and so is his style.

Will there be animals in Heaven? Will my dead cat be there?

The simplest answer I know to this question, so frequently asked by children, is: Why not? Children's questions are usually the best ones, and we should beware treating them with any less seriousness than their askers have in asking them. Right now, pets, like everything else in this world, can mediate God's love and goodness to us and train us for our union with him, or they can distract us from him. In Heaven, everything mediates and nothing distracts.

Will our bodies be clothed in Heaven?

Those who claim to have caught some glimpse of people in Heaven, whether in a vision or in a near—death experience, usually say that the people in Heaven are clothed, but differently than we are. The clothing is not artificial and concealing, but natural and revealing. Clothing came after the fall, to conceal what was shameful only because it was fallen. Once redemption is complete and the fall wholly reversed, nothing is shameful. Clothes will then be a pure glory, not half glory and half shame, as they now are. Perhaps they will seem to grow out of the resurrection body itself rather than be put on from outside.

Will there be music in Heaven?

Indeed. Even now, great music seems like an echo from Eden, a souvenir, a memory from Paradise—something not merely pleasant but profoundly meaningful in an ungraspable way, a high and holy mystery. Once again I refer (only as a clue) to numerous visionaries who have said they heard music in Heaven, but of such a different quality from earthly music that it was incomparable—like comparing a toddler's banging on a toy xylophone with a symphony orchestra.

Will there be time in Heaven?

Eternity does not mean simply endless time; that would be boring. Nor does it mean something strictly timeless; that would be inhuman. Time is part of our consciousness, and God does not tear up his plan for us; rather, he fulfills and transforms it.

I think eternity will include all time, as the dying see their whole life pass before them in perfect temporal order, not confusion, yet instantaneously. There is nothing more natural and all-pervasive in this world than time. Not only our bodies but our souls as well are immersed in time. Yet we complain about it. C. S. Lewis asks, "Do fish complain of the sea for being wet? Or if they did, would that fact not strongly suggest that they had not been, or were not destined always to be, aquatic creatures?" We long to step out of the sea of time onto the land of eternity, even though we do not really understand what eternity is!

What age will we be in Heaven?

Medieval philosophers usually thought we would all be 33, the ideal age, the age of maturity, as of Christ's earthly maturity. I take it this is symbolically accurate: we will all be fully mature. Infants who die prematurely will be given, by God (perhaps through the mediation of their own parents!), all the maturing they missed on Earth.

In Heaven no one will be old. Yet in a sense everyone will be both old and young, as a reflection of the God who is the Alpha and Omega, oldest and youngest, "beauty ancient yet ever new." Even now we sometimes see the wisdom of old age in the musing face of a baby or the eternal freshness of youth in the twinkling eyes of the very old. These are hints of Heaven.

Will there be privacy in Heaven?

I think not. No one will want to hold anything back, for no

one will be ashamed or afraid of being misunderstood or unloved. Privacy is like clothes and like laws: necessary only because we are fallen. When sin is gone, all hiding will be gone.

Will we be free in Heaven? If so, will we be free to sin? If so, won't anyone ever exercise that freedom?

In heaven we will not sin because we will not want to. We will freely choose never to sin, just as now great mathematicians do not make elementary mistakes, though they have the power to do so. In Heaven we will see the attractiveness of goodness and of God so clearly, and the ugliness and stupidity of sin so clearly, that there will be no possible motive to sin.

In Heaven, in the "beatific vision" of God, overwhelmed and filled with the total joy of goodness, baptized with goodness as a sunken ship is filled with water, no one could possibly ever want to turn from this perceived glory. Now, "we walk by faith, not by sight"(2 Cor. 5:7). Heavenly sight will not remove our freedom. Ask the blind whether sight would remove their freedom.

How do you get to Heaven?

This is the most important question anyone can ask. The answer has already been given: It is free. "Let him who is thirsty come, let him who desires take the water of life without price" (Rev. 22:17). Faith is the act of taking.
It sounds crazy, too good to be true. But it makes perfect sense. For God is love. Love gives gifts, gives

itself. God gives himself, his own life, membership in his family. We are made "partakers of the divine nature" (2 Peter 1:4).

God is pure love and pure love has no mixture of stinginess in it.

Is Jesus the only way? (Or can good pagans, Hindus, et cetera get to Heaven too?)

The game of heavenly population statistics is one that Christ discouraged his disciples from playing. When they asked him, "Are many saved?" he answered neither yes nor no but said, "Strive to enter in" (Luke 13:24). In other words, mind your own business, your own salvation, rather than speculating about others and statistics.

God has not told us the answer to this question, for his own good reasons, just as he has not told us when the world will end, another question about which we love to speculate. I think that in both cases we can see the wisdom of not telling us. If we knew when the world would end, we would not be ready at all times for the thief who comes in the night, unexpectedly. If we knew that most were not saved, we would tend to despair; if we knew that most were saved, we would tend to presumption.

JESUS:

Instead of thinking about your Loved One's body ending, think about not only what he/she is experiencing now, but what you will. If you think all that you have just read is what heaven will be like you are mistaken.

You can't even imagine what it is like, but I want you to start spending more and more time imagining what it will be like, especially what you will be doing and experiencing with all your loved ones.

What's more is you will have no memory of all that you suffered here. So use your imagination and let the kingdom of heaven I have prepared help to heal your grief.

CHAPTER 16
A GIFT FOR YOU FROM KEATON AND MARY GRACE

Keaton Paro is 9 years old and in 3rd grade. My only claim to fame is that she is my adopted grand-niece. Keaton and her family have been and are one of the great blessings the Lord has given me.

When she was 5 years old she really took to my older brother Fr. Fred Pompei. Every time she saw him she would run to him for his big hug.

My brother, who my sister Trish and I loved and love very much, was a holy man. Earlier in this book, my sister described my brother's graduation from his body that was a very painful experience watching him drift away.

When Keaton got the news she cried, and a couple days later my sister and I received a call from my adopted niece, Kara, Keaton's mother. She said she went into

Keaton's room and saw her kneeling and talking to someone. When she asked her who are you talking to, she said, "Fred".

So her mother asked her what he said and Keaton replied,

"I told him that I really miss him and asked him what heaven was like."

He said, "It's really beautiful here and I know a lot of people. I'm really happy and that he would watch over me and all the people he loves."

I wonder if that's why Jesus said, "Unless you become like little children you will never enter the Kingdom of Heaven."

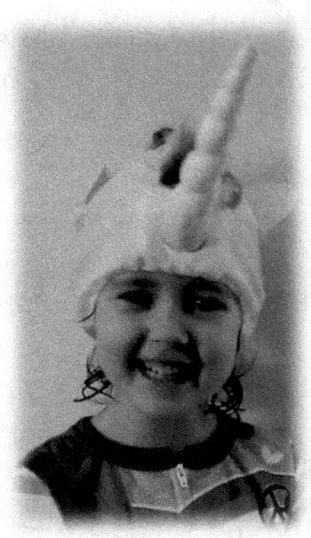

MG

Around thanksgiving I was really missing my brother. One night when I was visiting my good friends, the Kuehners, I was telling them how I really missed my brother, especially seeing and hugging him. They have 5 wonderful children and their youngest daughter's name is Mary Grace who I nicknamed MG. Well, MG who is in Kindergarten, must have been listening because she came over to me and said, "Fr. Pompei, you can touch him!" So I asked her, "MG, how can I touch him?"

She said, "Do what I do. Just close your eyes and imagine your brother right in front of you, then reach your hand out and touch him."

So, since that day, I took MG's way of feeling my brother's presence and when I really miss seeing, hearing, and embracing him, I close my eyes, picture him in front of me, reach my hand out and talk to him.

It really helps me when I miss him and want to talk to him like I use to.

Maybe **Keaton** and **MG's** gift to me is for you too!

CHAPTER 17
TIME WITH JESUS PRAYERS COMPILATION

(To help you locate those prayers in this book to become aware of Jesus with you every step of the way and in the future)

PRAYER WHEN YOU ARE OVERWHELMED

Evil is attacking you as it did me on the cross and when my good friend Lazarus' physical body died. Evil is tempting you to doubt that I am with you and doing nothing to help and your fear and suffering will never end.

Calm down and let me help you, and together we will stop the vicious circle.

Slowly Repeat My Words, and let them relax your mind and body little by little, so you can focus on just being here with me, just you and me...

- Be Still and Know that I am God.... (Pause 30 sec close your eyes)

- Be Still and Know that I am... (Pause 30 sec close your eyes)

- Be Still and Know... (Pause 30 sec close your eyes)

- Be Still... (Pause 30 sec close your eyes)

- Just Be... (Pause 30 sec close your eyes)

Trust me now, by praying these words **slowly** with all your faith, mind, and Soul.

- **"Your power, Jesus, is greater than the powers of Evil and Lies that are attacking me."**

- **"In Your name, Jesus, and by the power of your blood, I bind and cast out Fear, Worry, Anxiety, Doubt and despair."**

- **"Evil, you have no power over me. I belong to Jesus"** (Pause 15 sec.)

- **"Lord, I'm tired and surrender everything to you. Give me peace of mind and Rest!"**

Imagine the Holy Spirit and my unconditional love is embracing you, because it is.

Close your eyes and enjoy peace of mind and rest. Just keep choosing to be here with me and think positive and good thoughts, like all the people who love you. There's no rush, so take your time. **Think of them one by one and enjoy their presence when you do...**

Now, no more thinking, no more praying... just **'Being'**... together... Me with you... and you with Me. (Take as much time as you need)

Welcome back. You did it."

I want you to seriously consider stop reading. Take a nap or do something that will capture your attention, something you like to do and enjoy. **DO IT, STAY IN THE PRESENT,** and leave your problems, fears, tomorrow and the future up to Me.

Now get to it and remember, I will be right here with you, whether you are aware of me or not, in case we need to deliver these evil thoughts again...

All your Worrying is a waste of time and will change nothing. By doing something you like to do and getting connected with people who love you is a necessary part of not only bringing you peace of mind, but life and joy.

Always remember, it's **LOVE** that dispels your Fear. So let people in and watch what happens. Now get to it and you can continue your reading later for more good news about how you and I can really help your family, loved ones, and especially those who are suffering and getting ready to graduate.

I love you... always have and always will.

VISITING YOUR LOVED ONE

If you think I have no idea what goes through your mind when you are on your way to visit your loved one who is suffering and whose body is dying, you are mistaken.

When I got word that my good friend Lazarus had died, it was an overwhelming feeling of emptiness, and now that I was in an earthly body knew for the first time what a broken heart felt like. Here were some of my thoughts, and my guess is some of them are yours.

- You will see their bodies in pain maybe and anguish in their face along with a certain fear in their eyes.

- You will never see them full of life, whole, and healthy again.

- You will never see their smile or feel their touch ever again that you have been so accustomed to.

- They will no longer be at your holiday table and hear the sound of their voice that emanated their presence, the presence of their physical body through which you touched, held and embraced.

- You will no longer have them at your family's special events and you will miss them terribly and don't want to think about it.

- There will be no more memories to create when they leave.

- It all feels so unreal and like I'm in a very dark space in my soul and there is no light at the end of this or a way out of it.

These were my thoughts and feelings when I got word that my friend Lazarus was dead. The result of downloading and thinking about them has and is most likely why you don't know what to do or say or how you can truly help your loved one through their suffering with Hope and Love.

Here are the Truths that will not only set you free from all the awful thoughts and feelings of not knowing what to do or say, but liberate your Loved One from their fears, give them the hope of what's really happening to them, Graduation and not death, and most of all feel your Love and you theirs.

- The minute the negative thoughts above enter your mind, say it, shout it, and if you have to scream **NO** to them, do it. Tell them you are no longer going think about them. Instead, say **"LORD"** and turn your attention to me, because that's where I am and have been waiting for you to call upon me.

- Then, remember what you have been taught, that you will **not** focus on what your loved one looks like, or if they are in a hospital, nursing home, or hospice, the machines, caretakers and any negative thoughts that keep attacking your mind.

- Look beyond what you see to what is unseen, that is the 'One you love' who is in this body. Their

Spirit, Soul, their Consciousness is totally intact whether they are alert, unconscious, or in a coma physically.

- Now, just be with, talk to them, and treat them as you would if they weren't suffering. This in itself will give them the comfort and assurance that they are OK in the present.

- After you share stories, ask them what are some of the thoughts going through their head and what they are feeling.

- Listen and discern what might be controlling their minds and attacking them: Are they afraid, worried, angry with God, guilty and feeling there is no hope.

- Share with them what I have taught you about fear, suffering, and death. Tell them the Truth and use my words to dispel the lies that may be frightening them.

- Next, get them connected with me right there with you, because that's what I'm waiting for you to do. The way to do this is to invite them to pray and talk to me.

- Bless yourself, then ask to be aware of my presence there with you. (Pause 10 sec. to give yourselves time for your mind to do this.)

"Lord it's good to be with you."

- Then pray and ask for healing and deliverance from fear of suffering and what's in their future.

PRAY:

"Lord, I pray and ask first for full and total healing for _____, a miracle and extraordinary healing.

Secondly I pray for full and total healing if it is going to take time, days, weeks, whatever. In the meantime I ask that you give patience, courage, and strength to endure any pain or suffering until they are healed. Give them faith and trust in you from the moment they are tempted to doubt and worry about their future.

I pray that you will bless all _____'s caretakers and give them the wisdom and gifts to help in _____ 's healing.

Lastly, for those things that will not pass away, I ask that you continually deliver, bind and cast out all those negative thoughts and lies that evil will attack them with.

Finally Jesus, you said that Love dispels Fear. I join my Love to yours Jesus, and all those who Love_____.

_____, open your mind and heart and experience the embrace of all of us and Jesus' Love for you.

(Pause for 15- 30 sec. while softly saying over and over, "Thank you Jesus")

Hold their hand, look each other in the eye and pray

the words I taught you. **OUR FATHER**... Amen!
Give a sign of peace, an embrace, a kiss and say,

"Remember_____, the Lord is right here and Loves you and so do I.

- Now just visit, talk, and tell stories.

- If they are unconscious or in a coma say, do all the above steps, because their Consciousness, Soul, and Mind understands everything you are saying and doing.

- If you want to stay longer and they are in a coma, sleeping, or unconscious, bring a book, music, sit next to the bed, hold their hand and read in a soft calming voice. Every once in a while, if appropriate, wet a face towel with cool water, fold it and put it on their forehead and even gently wash their face and neck. Doing these things will let them know they are not alone and you and the Lord are still there with them.

- So, stay in the present with your loved one and enjoy them.

"I will never abandon you, so Trust and never abandon me."

-

BE MY VOICE FOR YOUR LOVED ONE

(To replace the thoughts that may be causing your loved one to be afraid or worried, read the Truth whether they are awake, unconscious or in a coma.)

PRAY:

Lord, you created me and gave me my voice. Use my voice to deliver _____ from any fears they may have, heal and give them hope and most of all know that they are not alone and that we love them.

I pray that you _____ will not hear my voice, but experience Jesus' voice not only speaking to you, but is right here and will walk with you through this. Lord, make me an instrument of your healing and hope.

- "Though you are walking through the valley of darkness, fear no evil, for I am with you."

- "Do not let your hearts be troubled. Have faith in God and have faith in me."

- "Your citizenship is in heaven where I created you. It is your home from where you came, and when you leave your body, I will take you home."

- "In my Father's house there are many dwelling places, not only for you, but for all those who believe in me."

- "I will change your lowly body to be like my resurrected and glorified body."

- "Your Sufferings of the present, as overwhelming as they are, are as nothing compared to the glory that I will manifest in you and for all eternity."

- "When I said while you are in the world and your physical body, you will suffer, but do NOT be Afraid because I am with you, I meant it. That's why I am with you now. What keeps you from experiencing it is your attention is on your suffering and what's happening with and around you.

- "Nothing will separate you from me, your Lord and your friend. Will anguish, or distress, or fear, or suffering? No, in all these things you are and will be more than conquerors because of my Love for you.

- Neither death, nor life, nor angels, nor principalities, nor present things nor future things, nor powers, height nor depth, nor any other creature will be able to separate you from the Love of my Father and me."

My brother and friend St. Paul spoke these truths, not because he believed in them but experienced them and me.

- "We who believe and are led by the Spirit are sons and daughters of God. You did not receive a spirit of slavery to fall back into fear, but received a spirit of adoption, because the God who created you is your Father and you are his son/daughter. If we are his children then you are his heir with

Jesus.

- So, join the suffering you are enduring with the sufferings of Jesus, for if you choose to suffer with Jesus you will be glorified with him."

Jesus, _____ and I love you because you loved us first. We choose to continue trusting you to guide and walk through this with you no matter what happens or what lies ahead. Heal those things that will pass away and give us the faith, strength, and courage to endure those that may not. AMEN!

FAMILY VISIT PRAYER WITH YOUR LOVED ONE

Jesus, it's good to be with you. We have come together as a family, to pray and ask you to heal and deliver us and _____ from our fears.

Help us to trust in you, and give everything to you now, so you can heal and deliver all of us from our fears.

Jesus, give us the grace to focus our attention on you, right here with us… (Pause 15 sec.) .

Lord, take all the negative thoughts, evil half-truths and lies that we have let into our minds, which are overwhelming us with worry and fear—fear that tempts us with doubt and even despair…take them right now, Lord. We give them to you…

Through the intercession of you, the Blessed Mother, St. Michael, and in the name of You, Jesus, our Lord and friend, deliver us from

- Fear, Doubt and Despair…   Bind and Cast them out
- Worrying about tomorrow   Bind and Cast them out
- Negative thoughts…   Bind and Cast them out
- Half Truths and Lies…   Bind and Cast them out

Instead, Jesus, we choose the TRUTH, that you are here with us. So give us the grace to not take any of these half-truths and lies back by thinking about or dwelling on them.

Replace our worrying about tomorrow and the future by staying in the present. (Pause 10 sec.)

Jesus, you said **love** dispels fear, so deliver our fears, not only with your love, but also by remembering all my family and the people who love me, believe in me and support me.

_____, You are not alone. The Lord and we, your family, are with you.

(Place your hand on your loved one and pray)

HAIL MARY... Amen.

OUR FATHER... Amen.

(Trace the cross with your thumb on_____'s forehead, then express your love for one another verbally or an embrace.)

Now enjoy your loved one, family and friends, and keep saying **'NO'** to the negative thoughts, half-truths, and lies.

Stay in the present, aware that I am and will be with you whether you experience me or not. You are not alone and neither is your loved one.

FAMILY PRAYER SERVICE TO GUIDE YOUR LOVED ONE
Through Graduation to Eternal Life

ORIENTATION
Spokes-person for family tells their loved one
(Whether they are conscious or unconscious)

- Who is there

- What's happening medically and spiritually
(According to Jesus)

Example:

"Dad, it's me Cathy your daughter, Joe is here and your grandchildren, Zach and Gabriela. We're here because we love you and don't want you to be alone.

Dad, what's happening is that you are in the hospital and there is nothing more that the doctors can do for your body, which means that your body is dying and you should get ready to graduate and leave it.

We are all devastated to hear this and then have to tell you. We're all frightened and in the state of shock as you probably are now. (After you cry and embrace)

The good news, Dad, is that we all have faith and know that when your physical body ends, at that moment, Jesus will raise you up and out of it and take you home to heaven where God created you.
Finally, you'll be free from all the suffering and fear your

body has caused you.

So Dad, we want to pray together with you and ask Jesus to guide and lead us through your leaving and our letting you go.

"Remember, as you watch your loved one leave their physical body, know that I am close by with him and waiting to set him free and take him home as you pray."

GRADUATION PRAYER
When your loved one is passing

(Make a copy of this prayer for each member of your family. At this moment pass them out and then begin)

ALL PRAY:

In the name of the Father, Son, and Holy Spirit, Amen.

Lord, we are here together with you as our family and friends. Help us to be aware of you right here with us, because you have been waiting for us to acknowledge that you are.

Jesus, you said to "Come to you all who are laboring and heavy burdened and that you would give us rest." _____ and all of us are heavy burdened and need to feel your presence and hear your words to lift us from sadness to Hope and Peace.

We'll take a few seconds to "Be Still" as the scripture says, to drop down from our thoughts and feelings into our hearts and very soul for the Holy Spirit, your unconditional Love, to fill this room and us. (Pause 15 seconds)

We love you Lord and it's good to be with you.

Negative and Evil thoughts are tempting and attacking us as they attacked you when your body was suffering and dying.

Tell us the Truth Jesus that will cast out those evil lies that this is the end of _____'s life and existence.

(Go around, take turns and be Jesus' voice for His words)

- "Peace be with you. It's me, Jesus, your Lord and most of all, your friend. I have heard all of your prayers and thank you for turning to and trusting me."

- "These are the moments that all of you have dreaded. You are experiencing what my blessed Mother did as she wept at the foot of my cross watching suffering and death destroy my body."

- "The World and Satan will tell you that death is the end of your life, nevermore to exist. This is a Lie and the reason I came, to destroy death once and for all, by raising you up from your physical body."

- "I am with you and have never left your side since you were born. If you are feeling alone and that I have abandoned you, so did I feel that way about my Father. In spite of my fear of the end of my life and feeling abandoned by my Father, I chose to Trust Him with my last breath.

_____, join your suffering and feelings to mine and Trust Me as I Trusted in my Father."

I tell all of you this, "The sufferings that you are experiencing now are as nothing compared to the glory I will give to _____ and all of you when I raise you up."

_____, your family and friends who are with me in heaven are more excited than you could ever imagine and waiting for your body to let you go and set you free. They already know what they will do when they see and embrace you. They are wondering what you will do, so start imagining and thinking about it.

_____, God **will dance** with **joy** when you are finally 'Home'.

So, stay the course. Console yourselves with the Truth that I really am with and will be with you in the days to come. Remember, Love conquers all things, so let's keep doing what we're doing, **loving one another**.

ALL PRAY:

Thank you Lord for the gift of our faith. Without it we would despair and be without hope, but you are that hope and it is the hope of eternal life that there are no words to describe. We love you Lord and want to thank you,

Response: **"Thank you Lord"**

Jesus" Leader:

- Jesus, for the gift of our faith... R. (All respond)

- For the Unconditional Love you had for us to endure your suffering and death... R.

- For your forgiveness of our sins, and loving us anyway when we do... R.

- For your words that speak the truth... R.

- For you, yourself, being that truth... R.

- For the great gift of_____... R.

- For blessing our lives with_____... R.

- For all the wonderful memories, you, _____, have given us... R.

(Each can share their own thanksgiving to the Lord by saying,)

"Jesus, I want to thank you for...."

Letting go:
Family members, one at a time are invited to express to your loved one,

- Your Love

- That you will miss them until you see them again

- Not to worry about you and let Jesus take them home

- Look for_____ when you get there.

- Personal expressions of your love

Guiding your loved one through what will happen:

1. (A family member or you if you are alone, help your loved one to 'let go' by describing what will happen, what to think, pray, and who to look for.)

2. Your senses will dim and no longer function. When it happens focus on the Lord instead. Don't try to fix them, and most of all say <u>NO</u> to the **Fear** that will tempt you like it did Jesus.

3. Look for Jesus, family members and your close friends who are already with the Lord.

4. Remember _____, _____, etc.

(All present describe to, whether they are conscious or not, stories and memories of the relationship they had with their family or close friends that you remember who have already graduated.)

- Keep doing this in your mind. This will help you focus on leaving your body and going to your real home where God created you, **finally, no more** suffering, pain and no more death, only the unconditional love of God.

- When you see Jesus and your loved ones with him, do whatever they tell you and go wherever they take you, and don't look back or worry about us. We'll be fine and take care of one another.

- Don't stop for anything or anyone else, just Jesus and your friends and family that you are now with.

- Until then, there's nothing to be afraid of. Your family who loves you is right here with you, and we're not going anywhere.

- Just keep focused on the Lord until you graduate by saying with your mind what Jesus said when his body was ending,

"Father, into your hands I commend my spirit"

_____, keep repeating Jesus words every now and then, until you see them.

END PRAYER:

ALL:
(Join hands with _____ or place your hand on them, and looking around at one another pray)

HAIL MARY, full of grace, the Lord is with you. Blessed are you among women and blessed is the fruit of you womb, Jesus. Holy Mary, mother of God, pray for us sinners now and at the hour of our death, Amen!

OUR FATHER...   AMEN!

(When you finish, one at a time, trace the cross with your thumb on your loved ones head, expressing your blessing and love. **After all finish**, express your love for one another, verbally or with an embrace.)

LASTLY, whether your loved one is conscious or

unconscious, share stories that you remember that the others may not have been part of.

Make sure you direct those stories not only to each other, but to your loved one whether they are conscious, semi-conscious or in a coma. Trust me, they will hear and understand everything, but may not be able to respond because their physical body is no longer functioning.

The good news is this will continue to keep you and your loved one focused on your love with them and dispel not only your fear and sadness, but more importantly your loved ones. In addition to this, they will experience they are not alone and surrounded by those who love them.

So keep telling stories and sharing with others who are there. Just hearing your voices and feeling your presence will be like seeing you stand and cheer for them as they start to cross the stage, get their diploma and graduate. (**COMMENCE** their new and **ETERNAL LIFE**)

PRAYER WHEN LEAVING THEM AFTER THEY HAVE PASSED

PRAYER

_____, it is so painful to look at your dead body, but we believe and know that you left it and Jesus raised you up and out of it. If you are still here in this room we love and miss you already.

Our only consolation is that you are no longer frightened and suffering. We hated seeing you that way and felt so powerless to help you and only wished we could take it away.

Jesus, grant us the grace to postpone our sadness and grief so that we can give _____ a great send off and celebrate the blessed gift of _____'s life to us, his family and friends.

_____, we really need you together with Jesus, to help us through these next few days to make arrangements for others to thank God for your life and grieve with us. Help us to make those necessary decisions for a service and your resting place, decisions that I know will be very difficult.

Jesus, as we leave _____'s body, we are saying '**Lord**' as you taught us so that we know that we are not leaving _____ alone, because he/she is with you in heaven and through the Holy Spirit you are with us. Amen.

(Embrace one another to console and heal each other's awful image of your loved one's lifeless body.)

VIEWING YOUR LOVED ONES BODY IN THE CASKET

(Open or Not, or in an URN, if cremated)

This is one of the things that you have probably thought about many times and dreaded when it would actually happen.

Well, it's happening and all the thinking about it and trying to prepare for it just doesn't seem to help.

The Truth is that it will be so overwhelming and numbing that you are already overwhelmed and you haven't even gone to the Funeral Home.

So, what to do:
Just before you enter the room or wherever they have been placed, say your Trust word, "**Lord**".

Become aware that the Lord is right there with you, because he knows you really need him and need him now.

As you approach your loved ones body, imagine the Lord is walking right next to you, because he is.

JESUS:
When Martha came to me and told me that her brother, my good friend Lazarus was dead, I wept with her and her sister Mary.

Then I asked them where have you laid him, and **together**, **arm and arm**, we went to the tomb where they had placed my friend. I know what you are feeling and the depth of those horrific images of your loved ones body when you first see them.

I wept bitterly as probably you will and that is good. Your tears express as mine did, how much we love them. Tears are also a gift that I gave you when you were created. They are the way to release all your fears, sadness, grief, but also the expression of the greatness of your love.

As you look upon your loved one, listen to me whisper in your ear,

"This is the body that they lived in, but they are not dead. I have already raised them from their body and taken them to Heaven, but their very Spirit that you love, is closer than you think."

A SHORT PRAYER BEFORE YOU LEAVE THE WAKE
(At the Casket or Urn Table)

LEADER:
Thank you Lord and _____ for being with us to get us through this wake service.

And thank you for all the wonderful people who loved you and will miss you. As you heal us, Jesus, heal them in the days to come.

We Love you _____ and we miss you so much already.

We want to really celebrate your life and give you a great send off at the funeral service.

Join us now from heaven _____, as together we pray,

HAIL MARY... Amen.

OUR FATHER... Amen.

In the name of the Father, Son, and Holy Spirit. Amen.

(Share an embrace of one another before you leave to console each other with your love.)

VISITING THE CEMETERY PRAYER
(With the Family and Friends)

LORD, BLESS THIS RESTING PLACE FOR _____'S EARTHLY BODY

Let us pray:

In the name of the Father, Son, and the Holy Spirit, Amen.

Lord, just as you wept at the site of your friend Lazarus's tomb. We too are overwhelmed with grief at the sight of _____'s grave.

We miss _____ beyond words. That's why we are here as his/her family and turn to you for healing and deliverance from the awful thoughts and images of his physical body dying and now in this grave.

Jesus, we have gathered here as _____'s family to experience our love for one another and _____.

Give us the grace to focus off the end of his/her earthly life and instead focus on you right here with us.

Lift us up from sadness to Joy with the knowledge that we were blessed to have _____ as a gift from you.

Lord, speak to us the Truth and give us the faith to believe that _____ is not dead but with you in heaven.

Reader:

"I am the resurrection and Life itself, when your earthly body dies, I will raise you up and out of it, like _____'s.

Remember this Truth when you are attacked by Satan and Evil's lies. Your earthly life is school and the death of your bodies is 'graduation' and 'commencement' of your new life.

Learn to believe and trust me, that the sufferings you are experiencing now are nothing compared to the glory I will manifest in you as I have in_____.

Call to mind and remember often, I love you, always have and always will."

PETITIONS: **Response: Thank you, Jesus**

Lord, thank you for the great gift of _____ in our lives... R.

Jesus, thank you for your resurrection that _____ now shares in... R.

Thank you for helping and us to overcome our fear of suffering and death... R.

Give us the strength to let go of _____ and enjoy his/her new life in heaven... R.

Grant _____ to experience freedom from all the pain and suffering from his/her earthly life... R.

You said that the sufferings of the present are as nothing compared to the glory you will manifest in us when we leave our earthly bodies. May _____'s glory be great in heaven, with no more tears, suffering and death... R.

In the days to come, Lord, heal our hearts and minds with the knowledge that we will see her/him again when we graduate, and on that day there will not only be no more death, but no more separation from our loved ones like there is now... R.

_____, we will continue to pray and talk to you and be open to signs and awareness that you are not far from us... R.

(A family member reads the following **from your loved one**)

IT'S ME _____

YOU PICTURE DEATH AS COMING TO DESTROY ME;
Picture instead Jesus took me to my real home, in heaven, where God created me.

YOU THINK OF DEATH AS MY LIFE ENDING.
Think of my new life as beginning and there are no words to describe what I am experiencing.

YOU THINK OF MY GOING AS A LOSS;
Think instead of what I have found; freedom from fear, suffering and Death.

YOU THINK OF ME AS PARTING FROM YOU;
Think rather that I have graduated and met God, who has always unconditionally loved me, and all the people I loved and love me who are already here with me.

YOU THINK OF ME AS LEAVING;
Think of me as arriving in heaven, because I have, and the Joy and Love I'm experiencing is greater

than anything I could have imagined like Jesus said.

SO, WHEN THE VOICE OF DEATH WHISPERS TO YOU, "YOU ARE DYING AND YOUR LIFE IS ENDING"; Hear Jesus voice and mine saying,

"You are graduating from your body and coming home with me, to be together forever." It's all **True**! I love you and will be waiting. Keep talking to me, because I'm not far from you and only your physical body separates us.

BLESSING OF YOUR LOVED ONES RESTING PLACE

Lord, we bless the resting place of _____'s earthly body. Through Your resurrection, we believe and know that he is not here, but with you.

On the Last day you will recreate a perfect body like yours for all of us, and there will be no more pain, suffering, and death; only the memories of our experiences of Love for one another.

Until we are all once again together forever, we bless your body's resting place and make it holy by the Love of Jesus and ours, your family. Amen!

(When Holy Water is available, all sprinkle and bless the resting place. If no Holy Water pray the following)

HAIL MARY... Amen

OUR FATHER... Amen.

FINAL PRAYER:

As we go our separate ways _____, we will miss you terribly and will console each other with the knowledge that we will see you again when we graduate. We promise to heal one another with the many funny and wonderful stories and memories you have given us. We love you _____. AMEN.

(If you remain, continue to share stories about your loved one and make sure you keep in mind while you are telling them that your loved one is closer than you think.)

A PRAYER BEFORE YOU BEGIN CLEANING THEIR ROOM
(For You, Family or Friend)

In the name of the Father, Jesus our Lord and friend, and the Holy Spirit, the Comforter, Amen.

Lord, this is a task that we have dreaded to do, so we are asking that we start by choosing to be aware that you are with us, because you said you would be.

As we go through belongings from their earthly life, give us the knowledge and grace of the truth, that they are NOT dead, but are with you and that they are not far from us, separated only by our physical bodies.

_____, it's us, your family and friends. As we go through your belongings, put memories in our minds that will reveal your love for us and your desire to heal our sadness.

If and when we cry and feel sad we want you to know it's because we miss you and love you.

So, together with you _____, we pray to you Father in the words you Jesus taught us to pray with.
　'**OUR FATHER**.... Amen.

"Thank you Jesus for my family, friends, and all those who love you."

A CLOSING PRAYER FROM THE CO-AUTHOR

My hope and prayer is that Jesus words and truth has guided and given you the wisdom and strength to endure yours and your loved ones pain and suffering, as he has mine.

Don't let anyone tell you how to grieve. We are all different. Cry until you can't cry anymore, and your tears will send the depth of your love to your loved one in heaven. And thank Jesus often for his suffering, death and resurrection and the hope you will see your loved one when you graduate.

I encourage you to deepen your relationship with the Lord by making a sacred place in your mind where you and Jesus can meet and walk together through anything and throughout your day. He is only one word away, and that word is **"LORD"**.

"The Lord is with you and me!"

Fr. Francis Pompei ofm

JESUS

From now on as I said many times when I walked the earth, "Do not let your hearts be troubled", so don't let yours. When you are overwhelmed and your heart is troubled, all you have to do is focus off what's causing it and say, **'LORD'**. I will be there because I have never left you.

Don't leave me here in this book and jump back into the world alone to deal with life that is subject to sin, problems, suffering, fear, and death. You have spent a couple hours reading and spending time with me, so keep doing it when you close the book.

Give me one half of your mind as the sacred place where we can meet and walk together like we did as you read. Thanks for not only believing in me, but trusting me. You have given me great Joy that you let me in, not only share in your suffering, but heal your spirit with Hope.

Remember, I believe in you and I Love you, always have and always will.

Keep talking to me when you close this book.

Whenever you miss us, your loved ones, know that we still love and miss you.

When you are tempted to believe and feel we are dead, we are not, and you will see us again for all eternity when you come home.

Until then, know that we are closer than you think, so pray and talk to us often.

Your loved ones and Jesus

"Lord, I trust you anyway"

THE TRUTH

*Life is School,
Death is Graduation*

*Graduation is
Commencement*

*Commencement is
Eternal life!*

Diploma

"Come Blessed of my Father, enter the Kingdom I have prepared for you"

CREDITS

- **EDITOR:** Trish Pompei, Sister of Fr. Francis Pompei ofm, and the late Fr. Fred Pompei, Diocesan Priest of Syracuse, New York, 53 years.

- **PETER KREEFT, What will heaven be like,** Thirty-five frequently asked questions about eternity.

- **DAVID**, Dealing with such a devastating loss; who wishes to remain anonymous

- **JILLIAN** , Famous Artist, Liverpool, New York, Contact: 'Have pen will create', Jillian.fabrizi@gmail.com

- **ANNIE HASLAM,** Going Home Song and Lyrics

- **NEW INTERNATIONAL BIBLE**

- **GRIEVING MYTHS AND FACTS**, www.heartachetohealing.com © Copyright by Heartache To Healing 2009

164

www.ingramcontent.com/pod-product-compliance
Lightning Source LLC
Chambersburg PA
CBHW070603010526
44118CB00012B/1441